25.6.

THE ANTI-ZIONIST COMPLEX

Jacques Givet

THE ANTI-ZIONIST COMPLEX

SBS PUBLISHING, INC.

First published in French under the title ISRAËL ET LE GÉNOCIDE INACHEVÉ by Librairie Plon, Paris.

©Librairie Plon, 1979.

English version by Evelyn Abel, revised and updated by Norman Langford and the author, © SBS Publishing, Inc., 1982.

All rights reserved. No part of this publication may be reproduced in any form or by any means without written permission from the publisher.

SBS Publishing, Inc.
14 West Forest Avenue
Englewood, NJ 07631

LIBRARY OF CONGRESS CATALOGING IN PUBLICATION DATA

Givet, Jacques.
  The anti-Zionist complex.

  Translation of: Israël et le génocide inachevé.
  Includes bibliographical references.
  1. Antisemitism—Addresses, essays, lectures.
  2. Jewish-Arab relations—Addresses, essays,
lectures.   I. Title.
DS145.G4513 1981   305.8'924   81-16693
ISBN 0-89961-019-6   AACR2
ISBN 0-89961-020-X (pbk.)

Printed in the United States of America

Contents

Introduction by Daniel Patrick Moynihan   vii

Foreword   xv

I   The Gesture and the Rest   1

II   Anti-Zionists and Other People's Jews: Moderates or Universalists   13

III   Anti-Zionists and Jews in the Other Camp: Extremists or Pro-Palestinians   37

IV   The Ways of Repression   65

V   Targets Missed   89

VI   Judaism and Edenisms   129

Introduction
by Daniel Patrick Moynihan

Introduction

During the 1970's, an especially blatant and vulgar brand of anti-Semitism became a unifying global ideology of the totalitarian Left. Couched in the language of opposition to Zionism, this anti-Semitism became the preferred vehicle of the Soviet Union and its clients in international forums for political assaults against the democratic nations—most obviously Israel, but ultimately all the West, and especially the United States.

"Anti-Zionism" was promoted by an intense propaganda campaign the Soviet Union had launched early in the decade, a campaign embraced and amplified by lesser radical regimes also hostile to the democratic West and equally anxious to undermine the legitimacy of the State of Israel. The Soviets had developed for this purpose a peculiar variant of Marxist analysis, arguing throughout the Third World that "imperialism", the supposed enemy of the new states, was in effect the creation of an international Zionist conspiracy. The clear implication was that Jews somehow played a special role in perpetuating the alleged injustices of international capitalism.

The connection was first made, according to Bernard Lewis, at the very dawn of the 1970's:

In a statement released to the press on March 4, 1970, a 'group of Soviet citizens of Jewish nationality'—making use of the facilities of the Soviet

Foreign Ministry—attacked 'the aggression of the Israeli ruling circles,' and said that 'Zionism has always expressed the chauvinistic view and racist ravings of the Jewish bourgeoisie.'

The notion was steadily elaborated and diffused in Soviet culture to the point where the October 10, 1980 issue of *Pionerskaya Pravda*, a tabloid-type weekly magazine for children aged nine to fourteen belonging to the Soviet youth organization, Pioneers, could run a feature that said:

> Zionists try to penetrate all spheres of public life, as well as ideology, science, and trade. Even Levi jeans contribute to their operations: the revenues obtained from the sale of these pants are used by the firm to help the Zionists.
>
> Most of the largest monopolies in the manufacture of arms are controlled by Jewish bankers. Business made on blood brings them enormous profits. Bombs and missiles explode in Lebanon—the bankers Lazars and the Leibs are making money. Thugs in Afghanistan torment schoolchildren with gases—the bundles of dollars are multiplying in the safes of the Lehmans and Guggenheims. It is clear that Zionism's principal enemy is peace on earth.

Predictably, this lie soon began to compel the Soviets abroad as well as at home. A steady stream of denunciations of Israel—frequently for embodying the Zionism the Soviets and their agents succeeded in labeling racism—came to be adopted at international conferences and meetings. The height of the campaign, though not nearly its end, came on November 10, 1975, when the United Nations General Assembly adopted the infamous Resolution 3379, declaring that "Zionism is a form of racism and racial discrimination". This marked a watershed in Soviet-inspired anti-Semitism; all that came later would build explicitly on this.

I tried to make this point at the time. I was then the Permanent Representative of the United States at the United Nations and I rose after the vote to say:

> Today we have drained the word "racism" of its meaning. Tomorrow terms like "national self-determination" and "national honor" will be perverted in the same way to serve the purposes of conquest and exploitation.

INTRODUCTION xi

And so, indeed, it went.

In 1978, Cuba, long a party to the campaign, became head of the "Movement of Non-Aligned Nations". Not coincidently, the next summit of heads of state and government of the Movement, convened at Havana between September 3 and 7, 1979, adopted a resolution affirming that

> racism, including zionism (sic), racial discrimination, and especially *apartheid*, constituted crimes against humanity and represented violations of the United Nations Charter and of the Universal Declaration of Human Rights.

It had become a crime to be a Jew who wished to return to the Jewish national homeland.

The only consolation, one could say, was that at least this had been voted in a forum where the United States and its principal allies were not represented, and so could not reasonably expect to sway the vote in favor of the legitimacy of a kindred democracy.

Yet, surprisingly, alarmingly, by the second half of the decade, the United States had already begun to abdicate responsibility in this regard, even in those arenas where it *could* influence the outcome.

Thus, on March 1, 1980, the U.S. voted in favor of a UN Security Council Resolution that found Israel to be in "flagrant violation of the Fourth Geneva Convention"—making it the first nation in history to be found guilty of violating the covenant that made illegal under international law the behavior of Nazi Germany.

Though this vote would later be disavowed, unconvincingly, by officials of the Carter Administration, the American willingness to acquiesce in Soviet-inspired attacks on Israel had been demonstrated. It would be confirmed on December 15, 1980 in the General Assembly when the U.S. abstained on a similar resolution reasserting Israeli violations of the Fourth Geneva Convention.

The irony and the tragedy is that, throughout, the Soviet campaign against Israel has been directed ultimately at the United States and the liberal democratic values on which it is founded. The adoption, by 1980, of a position of almost total American acquiescence in the campaign against Israel has done nothing so much as set the stage for subsequent attacks on the United States.

First they would attack Israel; then the United States, for its support of Israel; finally, the language of international politics would be directed against the United States itself.

Thus, the Non-Aligned Countries would issue a communique, following a meeting of Foreign Ministers and Heads of UN Delegations in New York on September 25th and 28th, 1981, replete—in the words of Ambassador Jeane J. Kirkpatrick—with "base lies and malicious attacks on the good name of the United States." It described an incident of August 19, 1981, wherein American planes above the Gulf of Sidra were attacked by Libyan fighters, as "aggression by the United States" and "a threat to international peace and security".

I brought the document to the attention of the U.S. Senate on October 14, saying:

> The United States cannot afford not to see the consequences of the language of politics in the world being turned against us. There is a real issue of language here, and this is totalitarian language.
>
> This language says, when you defend yourself against attack, you are declared to have been an aggressor. That is a standard Orwellian inversion of meaning. When you attempt to resist the aggression of others, you are said to be the aggressor.
>
> Likewise there are no Libyan troops in Chad. There are no Soviet troops in Angola. There is only American aggression in the Gulf of Sidra.
>
> The issues here are transcendent. They go beyond the events of the moment. They go to this question: Does the language of politics become that of totalitarian powers? Does its purpose become what we encountered at the beginning of the 1920's to pervert meaning, to reverse meaning, to corrupt meaning, to make the language inaccessible save to those who understand the code?

This is what comes of ignoring, or rationalizing, anti-Semitic propoganda and anti-Zionist attacks on Israel in international forums. Language is perverted to serve the purposes of freedom's enemies. This is where we are today.

As I wrote in an article for *The New Leader* in November 1979,

> It would be tempting to see in this propaganda nothing more than bigotry of a quite traditional sort that can, sooner or later, be overcome. But the anti-

Israel, anti-Zionist campaign is not uninformed bigotry, it is conscious politics. We are dealing here not with the primitive but with the sophisticated, with the world's most powerful propaganda apparatus—that of the Soviet Union and the dozens of governments which echo it. Further, this fact of world politics creates altogether new problems for those interested in the fate of democracies in the world, and of Israel in the Middle East. It is not merely that our adversaries have commenced an effort to destroy the legitimacy of a kindred democracy through the incessant repetition of the Zionist-racist lie. It is that others can come to believe it also. Americans among them.

Americans need to be better informed about the totalitarian threat, and the manner in which anti-Semitism and anti-Zionism contribute to it. And therein lies the reason for this English edition of *The Anti-Zionist Complex*: to enlighten Americans to the real nature, and the purposes, of the Soviet-sponsored anti-Zionist campaign. An outstandingly thorough work of original scholarship, Jacques Givet's analysis will become a standard reference on this most important of subjects.

Daniel Patrick Moynihan

Washington, DC
December 15, 1981

Foreword

It has never been easy to speak of the people of Israel or of the Jewish question, or indeed to be a Jew. This is a permanent condition, to which recent and contemporary events give further intensity. If someone has escaped genocide by a miracle—as I did, by jumping off a train of deportees, at a time when all my kith and kin had been gassed—such a person acquires a subjective and less than impartial view of the episode in question. So I am telling my own story, as well as that of the Jewish people. This may seem presumptuous, but also requires humility; the publicist's "I" can make demands and bear responsibility for what is said, but cannot take the place of that other, private ego which has its own vision of things. Furthermore, there are individual heroes at every level. The history of war includes Joan of Arc and Napoleon, but also Mrs. Miniver and the Good Soldier Schweik. So the Jewish story could and should be that of Everyman.

To say that I am a Jew, addressing non-Jewish readers, is not to detract from our common quality as human beings. It does mean that we cannot exchange destinies. But still, one writing and the other reading, we can explore a reality which to me is all the more palpable in that I feel it continuously threatened, and not only in the sense that any reality is subject to change. For the threat is directed against the essential quality which has brought my people—though at what a cost!—through pogrom and ghetto. By a dialectic which is that of life itself, this same quality helps to make me, as an individual, ever more alive and ever more free. Hence, if it comes to the point, I ought to be free to reject either Judaism or Israel, or even both, just as a Roman Catholic should be able to question his faith or a Frenchman to become a Cuban or anything else.

But this freedom becomes mine only if I can escape from the constraints of the Diaspora, only if I no longer depend on the goodwill, the generosity, the indifference, or the political scheming of others, of those who claim absolute power over me because, as a French Gaullist minister once actually said, I am "camping" in their country, and hence presume to persecute, change or tolerate me as they see fit. Or even to sing my praises: "How intelligent are the Jews!"—the French Catholic writer Jacques Maritain once exclaimed. It may seem churlish, but I must decline this gracious compliment. In Israel, a Jew is on exactly he same footing as anybody else. He is no longer always submerged by an alien majority. He feels no need to display special intelligence or that sharpness of wit which Jews are traditionally supposed to have developed in hostile surroundings. Living in Israel, the Jews enjoy the right to their own quota of fools, or of any other class of people, and feel no particular shame or pride about it. This is because they now possess a permanent sense of identity, no longer at the mercy of shifting and incoherent events.

I am a Jewish writer expressing myself in French; I am not a political animal, nor have I been trained in, or bear the impress of, any particular school of thought. Before the horrors of fascism, which lives on under various names, descended on us during this century, my personal tastes inclined me towards the exploration of Beauty in its various forms, especially, perhaps, the more recondite; towards study, which dispels ignorance and reinforces doubt; but also towards the seductions of that perverse form of freedom we call idleness, no doubt because we are too lazy to invent another name.

So I preferred poetry and its emotions to dry political treatises. I called myself a poet and was appreciated as such by some. Although sensitive to lack of fame, this was not so much because I resented obscurity as because I was forced to recognize that poetry might be rather inane. Hence I was not prepared for polemics, an art which requires cultivation of the studied frown and of venom at command, together with mastery of an armoury ranging from withering sarcasm to the quiet sneer. What induced, or rather forced, me to try my hand at it was the fact that after the war of June 1967,[1] so many people, in speaking of us, of me, began to see red,

---

[1] My essay *La Gauche contre Israël?* ("The Left Against Israel?") appeared in April 1968.

or stopped seeing straight at all. Among these were some Jews whose vision was—and still is—very uncertain. It is never easy to be oneself; when a man's sense of identity and his awareness of himself as a Jew are at loggerheads, the result is liable to be confusing, even distressing. For Jews in this position, the emergence of Israel on the scene has intensified their inner conflicts.

Having decided to defend the cause of Israel—people and nation—in the Diaspora, without joining any organization or party, Zionist or other, so as to preserve my freedom of judgement, I prefer to call myself simply "pro-Israeli." But this is no time to play on words, when the enemy is juggling with them for his own purposes. Does he think to wound me by calling me "racist"? Verbal counterfeiting is too widespread today for me to refuse him this low trump card in a deck in which all the cards are marked. But it would be dangerous to assume that some cards are less bad than others. All should be swept from the table. Furthermore, the more blatant the cheating, the easier it will be for me to combat it.

The task is hard, and for a reason which at first sight may seem of minor importance but emerges as soon as one starts to write. The author who, wishing to be Jewish and alive, is naive enough to think that such an ambition needs no explanation finds his assertion of identity constantly impugned. Neither his words nor his intentions are understood. He has continually to start afresh, as though the ground had never been cleared. Like the false Messiahs with which Jewish history is studded, he comes before his time. I realize that a book is not enough; a question such as that raised here cannot be confined within its pages. Stuff them with digressions and parentheses, bolster them with references and footnotes, garnish them with subtitles, it will be of no avail. The matter overflows on every side.

The task is hard for another, more serious, reason. Because of the capital importance I attach to the reality of Israel, I have to be exacting towards those who direct that country's destinies. Had I chosen to praise Israeli policies without discrimination, these pages could have followed a path marked out in advance, but I might have found myself in a rut. I have preferred to run the risk of not satisfying anyone completely.

Furthermore, it requires a certain audacity, or presumption, to seek to make one's voice heard amid the din created by the information with which we are bombarded on every side, and especially so at a time when language is deliberately used to mislead.

This book was written in the hope that it would meet a need, namely, for someone to speak out loud and clear. But it also seeks to be an essay in political philosophy. I may have been too ambitious, but without ambition I could never have completed the task I had set myself.

J. G.

THE
ANTI-ZIONIST
COMPLEX

The Jews have no scruples. They respect no religion other than their own and betray the countries which grant them asylum. . . . Public opinion began by condemning Hitler's anti-Semitic policies. Today, the world realizes that he was right and that there was a logical reason to build the crematoria, so as to chastise those who display such sovereign contempt for humanitarian principles, religion and law.

—Amin Mansoor, *Al-Akhbar*, Cairo,
19 August 1973

A few of us, left-wing Jews, were deterred from espousing the Palestinian cause by the unmistakably anti-Jewish undertones of pro-Palestinian speeches and writings.

—Pierre Goldman, *Libération*, Paris,
31 October 1978

I
The Gesture and the Rest

On 26 March 1979, a peace treaty between Egypt and Israel was signed in Washington, D.C., by President Anwar Sadat of Egypt and Prime Minister Menahem Begin of Israel—an endorsement of the efforts which had led to the Camp David Agreement of 17 September 1978 and one of the steps towards peace in the Middle East provided for therein.

Between these two dates, the 33rd General Assembly of the United Nations, in New York, and the 15th UNESCO General Conference, in Paris, had continued their deliberations, marked as usual by virulent attacks on Israel, without investigation or due process of law, for alleged heinous crimes.

There are thus two parallel roads leading to entirely different goals. The first was inaugurated by the Sadat-Begin meeting on 19 November 1977. Where it will lead even the protagonists themselves do not really know. The other road, designed to lead to a specific end, is that chosen by those who have noisily resurrected an old bogey under a new name: "Zionism." The crucial date here is 10 November 1975, the climax (but neither the beginning nor the end) of a campaign waged by the Soviet Union and its satellites, together with the Arab countries and their customers, who when it comes to condemning Israel regularly impose their will on the United Nations and then become the "international community." On that day, 10 November 1975, the General Assembly solemnly ruled that Zionism was "a form of racism." Behind that resolution lies a scandalous conspiracy, a hoax, which I shall denounce and try to explain. To begin with, let us examine the significance of the first of these two roads, narrow and beset with obstacles though it be.

Sadat's Gesture

On 19 November 1977, the Head of State of the most important Arab country set foot in a land hitherto always referred to (if mentioned at all) in the Arab world as the "Zionist entity." He was received with full honours and deep understanding. Such moments are in every sense historic, becoming part of the national legend. Thus, in France, the fall of the Bastille on 14 July 1789 remains forever engraved in the memory of Frenchmen, and the subsequent Restoration of the French monarchy is hardly remembered, except by historians. Like the fall of the Bastille, President Sadat's visit had immediate political consequences.

First, it meant Egyptian recognition of the reality of Israel. The actual words used, or the gloss put on them, matter little. "I think, therefore I am," wrote Descartes. "You came to see me, therefore I must exist." No matter what the future may hold, that first handshake between the President of Egypt and the Prime Minister of Israel will always symbolize one thing to which Israel aspires, namely, direct contacts between responsible leaders at the highest level, as a prelude to negotiations and peace. At one stroke, politics took the place of demonology. One short phrase, with the verb in the past tense, stands out from President Sadat's speech in the Knesset: "We always used the words 'so-called' when referring to the State of Israel." In all probability these are the words which Israel's enemies, now his own, will find it hardest to forgive. Uttered beneath the portrait of Theodor Herzl, the official founder of Zionism, from a rostrum adorned with a seven-branched candelabrum, the emblem of Israel, they have a double significance: they acknowledge a fact and also that errors have been committed in the past, and they constitute a kind of commitment to the establishment of links between the two countries. The first of these links is already forged. A road had been blocked; it is now open. It is as though a breach had been made in the Berlin Wall.

There is every reason to rejoice at President Sadat's refusal to be deflected from his chosen course. In taking his decision, he appeared in a new and radically different light; at all events, he presented a marked contrast to his predecessor Nasser. But there is no guarantee that his feelings will remain unchanged.

Nor—and this is more serious—can there be any certainty about the sentiments of the man who will one day succeed him. Islam, especially since the fall of the Shah of Iran, has become far more militant. What other Arab leaders, and the men in the Kremlin, think has been made very clear. Thus Egypt's recognition of Israel is the more precious for being fragile. There is a Swedish film in which the heroine, after many vain attempts, catches a butterfly; the moment she does so, a shot rings out, and she falls dead. May Heaven preserve us from an assassin's bullet.

There is an extraordinary contrast between this bold but nevertheless limited gesture of political realism on the part of Egypt and the storm of indignation and alarm which swept the Arab world (especially the Arab countries with dictatorial governments) as a result. What is striking is the continued existence of a fund of bitter, hitherto intractable, and often hysterical hatred. Note, in this connection, the behaviour of the Iraqis at the Tripoli meeting on 5 December 1977, when they walked out to signify that for them a condemnation of the Egyptian move was not enough, and to out-trump in lack of moderation the most extreme among the leaders of the PLO.

The Egyptian gesture, then, appears extraordinary only by contrast with this persistent hatred. Did it, however, as is often affirmed, constitute a unilateral concession by Egypt? Certainly, it meant a radical break with past policies. We are told that Israel must make real concessions in return. But it is surely inconceivable that, in exchange for a decision by a former enemy at last to recognize its existence, Israel should offer concessions of a kind and magnitude which would jeopardize its security, even existence. As Israel sees it, President Sadat's gesture, magnanimous or miraculous as it may appear, represents no more than an end to blindness, even though the will behind the gesture was something to rejoice at. To demand excessive concessions in return is to ask Israel to accept security risks which would be accepted by no other State, as a glance at the map will reveal. Imagine what the response would be if, in negotiations with the United States, the Soviet Union were asked, for the sake of *détente*, to withdraw its forces from just one of the European countries invaded or annexed from 1940 onwards in the sacred name of national security. The discussions between Egypt and Israel, thus happily inaugurated, are proceeding with their ups and downs, but can continue only if a certain balance is maintained between the two parties.

The rejectionists, in the meantime, continue to talk to themselves, while condemning Israel, whose existence they deny, for its failure to respond. The

4   THE ANTI-ZIONIST COMPLEX

incendiary language they employ will undoubtedly continue to have its impact on opinion, blurring people's perception of political realities and resurrecting demons still imperfectly exorcized.

The fact remains that today, recognized as existing (if still the adversary), no longer a phantom invariably qualified by the expression "so-called," Israel is under an obligation to respond.

For today, after two thousand years of dispersion and a fight for survival lasting more than thirty years, the Jewish nation enjoys freedom of choice. The dispersal was enforced by Roman arms (which did not prevent some Jews from taking it lightly). Similarly Zionism, though invested by many Jews with a national or spiritual significance, was readily accepted by others who saw no alternative open to them. Again, in this century, the Zionist pioneers had no desire to wage war or to dominate others, in so far as this was not essential to their survival. In the last resort, their one ambition, for themselves and their children, was to stay alive, no longer to be arbitrarily massacred or persecuted as stateless persons, no longer to be "protected" or tolerated. The road is now open, but those concerned must have the will and the ability to keep it so; otherwise the opportunity will be lost, perhaps forever.

Let me be clear. It would be vain and pretentious to offer advice to the government of Israel as to any specific steps it ought or ought not to take. On the other hand, an observer outside the country may well have a clearer view of the climate of opinion abroad. For the political armoury of Israel (contrary to widely accepted opinion) has always been weak in the sphere of public relations. Israel does not go in for self-advertisement. Here the enemies of Israel, led by the PLO, have been more adroit. From the outside, it is perhaps easier to discern failings such as rigidity, lack of initiative, or simply indifference; and if so there may be a right, and even a duty, to offer criticism and advice.

Persistence of the Rest

This is all the more so because the anti-Zionist resolution adopted by the United Nations on 10 November 1975 is still producing effects. There has been a new development: the Arab rejectionist countries and the Soviet bloc now match their attacks on Israel, a hundred times repeated, with condemnation, sometimes vigorous, of Egypt's new line. Thus, President Sadat's decision will at the worst provide a respite; at the best, a foundation for dreams of a better future, perhaps even for specific action to make these dreams come true. But even at the best (assuming some kind of understanding is reached), hostilities will continue, perhaps in a new guise, simply because the ambitions of Israel's hard-line enemies have not been given full satisfaction. With regard to Jerusalem, especially, an ideological and religious campaign will attempt to fan ancient prejudices and hatreds and enlist them under the banner of anti-Zionism. Field Marshal Amin Dada would undoubtedly enter the lists were he still directing the fortunes of a member State of the United Nations. Speaking to the Ambassador of the Soviet Union, who apparently heard him out without dissent, he declared that Hitler had been wrong in not wiping out the Jews altogether.[1] Such an enormity would hardly be worth noting were it not that such statements do seem to have certain political effects. In July 1976, at Entebbe, this distinguished soldier was an accomplice in the taking of hostages and helped in singling out the Jews. The hostages were of course rescued, thanks to the skill and audacity of Israeli forces, and the episode later became the subject of several films, the showing of which was forcibly prevented in several European countries by anti-Zionists and their sympathizers.

More recently, for three whole weeks in November 1979, Moslems were at each other's throats at a site above all others sacred to their faith, in the very heart of Islam. If only the incident could be dismissed with the thought that there are fanatics everywhere, and that the matter is of no concern to us. But this we cannot do, for Khomeini and his followers have implicated us. We, the infidels, the unbelievers, must one day be brought into the fold by holy war. In Teheran as in Islamabad, a rumour, though fantastically improbable, sufficed to unleash the mob against the "Zionists," accused of having instigated the unhappy events in Mecca.

The Western public knows very little about either Arabs or Jews and is readily swayed. It would be a mistake, therefore, to underestimate the effects of anti-Zionism thus exacerbated. The more extreme and determined anti-Zionists provide the killers of Jews with aid and succour, offering shelter and procuring arms, identity cards and travel documents. The most pernicious of all are those intellectuals who offer a ready-made ideology. Thus, the concept of a "secular" Palestine to succeed Israel is of European, not Arab, origin, the idea of a secular State being totally alien to Moslem doctrine and tradition.

[1]*Le Monde*, Paris, 14 September and 12 October, 1973.

6 THE ANTI-ZIONIST COMPLEX

After the Nazi attempt at total extermination in the 1940s, it might have been expected that Jews would at least be acknowledged to possess a right to life. But no, this right, and the right to live as a Jew, has been unceasingly challenged from all sides, and it is always the Jew who is called upon to explain why he should be allowed this double privilege. A man can be a Jew, but he does not belong as of right to a nation once more emerging on the stage of history with the same rights as any other. The maneuvers here are legion, ranging from bad history and legal quibbling (and the Jew has no right of reply) to the occasional massacre, should opportunity arise.

This, then, is what I refer to as the "rest"—impermeability to argument, condescension, and, above all, refusal to admit the legitimacy of a Jewish State, to allow it to attain its natural dimensions, to grant it the right of self-defence. The Jewish State is expected passively to undergo attack, never to hit back, and certainly never to attempt a preventive strike. Or—a supreme refinement—it must rely for its defence on others. A Jewish State which refuses to bow to what others think good for it, and declines to be condemned in accordance with criteria it has had no part in shaping, is a cause for scandal, even though it be the Jews themselves who will pay the price for imprudent surrender to objurgation. Hostility to Israel, whether unconscious or deliberate, outspoken or dissembled, ultimately derives from a refusal to accept a Jewish national entity, the existence of which is stubbornly opposed in the name of some abstract universalism or on behalf of some other national movement. Or perhaps both grounds of objection are invoked at the same time; the censurers of Israel seem untroubled by inconsistency.

A nation absent from history is liable to find itself the victim of events. The reemergence of Israel—an event so unexpected as to appear miraculous—has given Jews an opportunity to become once more masters of their own collective fate and to retrace the steps which led their forefathers into exile. But the glory of that event has been a deeply alarming experience for certain Jews (among whom anti-Zionism has found eager allies) too long accustomed to the gloom of the Diaspora and its twilight delights.

Human lives must never again be bargained for against something else. Under Nazism, trucks were offered in exchange for Hungarian Jews (and the bargain was refused). Recently oil has emerged as a bargaining counter of immense power. But the analogy is superficial and misleading. Nor is it admissible to indulge in gloomy reflections and to seek consolation in the thought that things are what they have always been, Israel being persecuted among the nations just as Jews have always been persecuted as individuals; such pessimism may induce a cowardly inaction.

But the existence of Israel makes all the difference, a fact of which the Soviet Jews (of all Jews, the most conscious of persecution) are well aware. Unlike the wretched prisoners at Auschwitz, who could not hope for rescue, Jewish hostages can now look to the strong right arm of the Israeli Army. An organized national community (beset with difficulties though it be), a sovereign State (although like other States necessarily limited in the exercise of its sovereignty) is vastly better than a continuation of the system whereby Jews were subject to the national jurisdiction of a score of different countries and often suspected of less than total national loyalty.

Human lives are not negotiable against trucks or oil. But negotiations to establish the peaceful coexistence of different States are perfectly legitimate. They are adamantly refused by the authors of the Charter of the PLO and those influenced by that notorious document, who are willing, at the most, to tolerate Israel only in so far as it is at their mercy or under their control.

The Other Problem

The problem of the Palestinian Arabs, which I wish to face squarely, has to be considered with an eye to all the realities involved, beginning with those of which, as a Jew, I am most intimately aware. It is more straightforward, and in the interests of both parties, to begin by stating one's own case.

The first point to inspire misgivings is that the PLO emerged as a political force at a time when there could have been no more effective instrument wherewith to encompass the destruction of Israel. Before 1967, when the West Bank was occupied by Jordan and Gaza by Egypt, there was no mention of the Palestinians, let alone of their "inalienable rights." At that time the Palestinian Arabs were very much the poor relations of their Arab brethren. But these poor relations, specialists in spectacular attacks by bomb and bullet, are to be pitied only in so far as a Jewish presence in this corner of the world (and no longer in the form of a minority) thwarts their ambitions. Such a Jewish presence the PLO (and a certain type of alienated Jew) cannot stomach.

According to Jewish tradition, life is the highest value of all. But even if, as I believe, Israel exists to guarantee the survival of the Jewish people, it will, like any other country, be far from perfect, and will certainly not live up to the very high ideals which some (for varying motives) would demand of it. There is no point in regretting that the grace of childhood disappears when the child becomes an adult. Nobody is entitled to demand that the State and people of Israel—alone—should sacrifice their existence on behalf of qualities which no State can possibly possess. If the living reality of Israel be contrasted with an ideal that has suicidal undertones, we cannot possibly doubt that Israel is right in pursuing its struggle for survival.

I have always hated war and violence, in which the ugly side of human nature gains the upper hand—the greed, the carnivorous jaws ready to bite, the moral cancer which may spread and devour men altogether. It would be naive not to recognize that on the whole force rules the world. But force can be deflected, influenced, and occasionally overcome by the passion for liberty, by imagination, by a thirst for justice. To this, the recent revolt by dissidents in the Soviet Union and Eastern Europe bears witness.

It is one thing to recognize that change—necessary and even beneficial—will inevitably be accompanied by a certain amount of violence; quite another to glorify violence for its own sake or as purifying those who practice it.

In a fight for national survival, it is unrealistic to overlook the existence of those who are thirsting for your blood. What distinguishes Israelis from the P.L.O. in the present context is that the former do not glory in the death of their opponents. For more than a quarter of a century now, Jews have been able to refuse a passive death—for them, a new and dazzling development, which should be taken in mitigation of any blindspots they may show. Another difference between Israel and its hard-line enemies is that Israel is prepared to consider, if not all possible courses of action, at least several, whereas the latter make no proposals and accept none, except such as would entail the complete or virtual disappearance of Israel.

I am an unconditional champion of Israel's right to exist, not merely (although this should be enough) because I want to go on living (and to go on living as a Jew). I believe that a people which has paid so very heavy a toll in blood and suffering has amply earned the right of self-determination, just as any other people. Moreover, owing as I do my life to a miracle, it is my duty to ensure that miracles of this kind will never again be required.

A *Matter of Permanent International Concern?*

Whenever I catch myself thinking that the Jewish problem is one of the central issues of our time, I have to remind myself that there are other matters equally deserving the world's attention. But I am not sure. To clear our minds, let us take an event of even greater historical importance than the Sadat-Begin meeting of November 1977, namely, the Allied victory over Hitler in May 1945. But in Poland, in less than thirty years . . . I hear indignant protests: "An extreme example. We all know the Poles acted ignobly; even the Left condemned them." Yes, indeed. Immediately after Hitler's bloodbath and the establishment of a socialist government in Poland, could anybody possibly have prophesied that within twenty-five years Jewish survivors of the Warsaw ghetto and the furnaces of Auschwitz, who had stayed in Poland rather than emigrate precisely because of their anti-Zionist sentiments, would be expelled for being Jews? Who could have imagined that these Jews would be accused, not of being too few in the higher reaches of the ruling party, but of being too numerous? Yet this, unimaginable as it may seem, is what occurred.

These same Polish Jews, who had fallen over backwards to be more Polish than the Poles, were forced to show greater loyalty to the government in power than any other group of citizens. Their zeal availed them nothing. Yet these were the very people held up as examples for Jews wishing to affirm their identity, as such: "X and Y, Jews like you, think like us; therefore you, Zionists, are wrong." But in the event of tension, should anything go wrong, then everybody knows where X and Y are to be found and what should be done with them. In such circumstances, as was the case in Poland in 1968, the authorities will go back to the eighteenth century to unearth ancestors of whom a man may have been totally ignorant, in order to confiscate his property overnight and drive him ignominiously into exile.

There was a great show of indignation in 1973 when Israel, taking up arms to repel attack, exercised the right of self-defence. Governments, including the government of Poland, accused her of being the aggressor on Yom Kippur Day; they had to eat their words a few days later, and glorify the real aggressors, who had in the meantime been boasting of their feats.

When the Third Reich, whose dominant ideology comprised a virulent anti-Semitism, collapsed in discredit, régimes based on entirely different values were installed in the countries it had overrun. Yet whenever these régimes run into difficulties, as any system of government is bound to do, it is all too clear that the old anti-Semitism is still very much alive. The prospective victims can never be sure that despite all apparent progress there will be no relapse into older, sinister patterns of behaviour. The persecution of the Jews in the Poland of the 1960s has a familiar air (French history, too, is full of such episodes, including the Dreyfus case and collaboration with the Germans in rounding up French Jews in 1942)

We are told, or it may be rumoured, that the action taken against these Polish Jews is to be relaxed or entirely annulled, which is equivalent to confessing that anti-Jewish action did take place. What guarantee is there that similar things will not occur tomorrow? Even assuming that the Sadat-Begin meeting has the most gratifying possible aftermath, it would be a bold man who would take a bet that anti-Semitism, in Poland or elsewhere, has been finally laid to rest.

It is the repeated emergence of the same old theme in different guises that needs elucidation. The language of anti-Semitism and anti-Zionism—blatant, insinuating, grotesque or vulgar—is monotonous enough, testifying more to the existence of a psychological malaise than to any originality of thought. Anti-Zionists range from the moderates to the extremists, who are not open to argument at all. Some of the most unbridled extremists, some of the most emotionally confused among the moderates, happen to be Jews; and the Jewish moderates, especially, are often held up for our admiration. Unfortunately, such persons tend to be the rejects and the dross of a community undergoing a transformation, a community of which they are very far from being representative.

The Jewish Diaspora is not immune to its own brand of wishful thinking, undue depression or elation, and mental confusion induced by misinformation. Its weaker members turn renegade or, like metal filings arranging themselves round lines of force, turn ingratiatingly to the powers that be, or what they see as such. That there should be Jews to challenge the existence of Israel and indulge in lengthy public self-questioning on this theme represents warped thinking, a breach of faith, and a human tragedy. And this is a unique phenomenon. No Algerian, Cambodian, Chilean, Czech (and now, Afghan) exile, however bitterly opposed to his current government, questions his country's right to exist.

I may be accused of giving unmerited importance to persons who have cut themselves off from the fate of their own community. But their views are often given exceptional publicity in quarters ill-disposed towards Israel, and hence they cannot be ignored.

It is not my intention to examine, one by one, the various cogs in the machinery of anti-Zionism; an encyclopedia would be needed. I shall limit myself to considering certain ways of thought, certain patterns of twisted thinking, which tend to pass unnoticed, especially in the field of international public relations, where Israel and her friends have been most timid in their reactions. It is here that the PLO and its sympathizers have landed more blows than they have received. I shall merely offer a few examples, chiefly from the decade 1967–1977, a period significant in that it marks the beginning of the anti-Zionist offensive unleashed after the 1967 war and takes us up to the initial contacts between Egypt and Israel, which represented a check to that offensive. I shall then broaden my inquiry and probe the deeper reasons for the drama in which the Jew, whether he likes it or not, is an actor.

It is important, certainly, that a Jewish State should have been recognized by that Middle Eastern country which had hitherto been its principal enemy. It is even more important to inquire why recognition should have caused such hesitation or embarrassment in quarters remote from Middle Eastern affairs. How does it come about that by their mere presence, irrespective of what they do (and even if they should do nothing), the Jews have so often been seen as a threat, sometimes to stability (by the champions of the *status quo*), sometimes to revolution (by revolutionaries)? Is it because the modern Israeli represents, *par excellence*, the Jew who has thrown off external constraints, refusing both persecution and patronage, that such obsessions should have been transferred to him?

Persecution, stubborn misunderstanding, faulty reasoning—such phenomena, baffling to the sociologist, are bound to interest me more intimately as a Jew and hence a potential victim. They cannot be due to accident or arbitrary malice. Their emergence at any particular time or place seems to obey no definite law (there are in fact none such in history), but does seem to coincide with impulses which manifest themselves in society from time to time. Why should they occur, and why should Judaism be invested with a false air of menace? These are the questions I shall attempt to answer.

II
Anti-Zionists and Other People's Jews: Moderates or Universalists

Extreme anti-Zionists refuse to recognize that the Jewish nation exists as such; for them, Israel is a non-State, the mere mention of which invites condemnation. Moderates, on the other hand, recognize that there is such a thing as a Jewish problem (even if, in their view, the Jews do not constitute a nationality as ordinarily defined). They admit that the State of Israel exists, but this is as far as they are prepared to go. Both extremists and moderates are politically unrealistic, but while the former are radically negative, the latter remain unable or unwilling to make up their minds.

Indecision in the Jewish moderate anti-Zionist is a sign of bewilderment. At the time when Zionism was taking form, various schools of thought were represented among the Jews of the Diaspora, but such was the optimism and liberalism of the early Zionists (themselves a product of the Diaspora) that these conflicting currents were tolerated.

The original dynamism of the Zionist movement was largely spent in the tremendous task of resurrecting a nation. Optimism waned and liberalism degenerated into slackness; in time, the Jews of the Diaspora began to think of Zionists as somnolent party hacks—*apparatchiks*—occasionally emerging from their slumbers to pass round the hat. The movement's extraordinary achievements no longer sufficed; Zionism had advanced at a pace that left its rear unguarded. Today, to fight its enemies and mobilize its friends, Zionism must urgently review its methods and activities, re-form its ranks, and see to its public image in the world at large. To leave the enemy to sow the land left fallow is to invite a poisoned crop.

I offer this criticism in an attempt to win over the moderate anti-Zionists, although with no great hope of success, for despite their mental confusion they remain by and large firmly under the spell of fashionable ideals: egalitarianism, universalism, concern for balance at all costs. To remain "objective" with regard to the Israeli-Arab conflict, they fall over backwards; for them, Israel is perpetually in debt to those who, however grudgingly, admit its right to nationhood. The roots of this attitude probably lie in the conviction that more can be demanded of Jews than of non-Jews; Jews cannot enjoy the same rights as others, or if they do, such rights must necessarily have been usurped.

Universalism

Universalists who recognize the existence of Israel while claiming for themselves the right to hold aloof fail to grasp what recognition implies, namely, secure frontiers (without which such recognition is meaningless) and the right to be different (without which it is artificial). The universalist who is a Jew into the bargain, torn between several options, lacking roots himself—a victim of history—cannot admit that the search for roots is a legitimate activity and becomes hopelessly confused.

It is true that the decision to fall in with one camp or the other is never easily taken. Life can continue almost indefinitely in the even tenor of its ways, as long as nothing unforeseen occurs to upset or destroy the framework which has rendered this possible. Take the war waged by the United States in Southeast Asia. How easy, straightforward and exhilarating the issues seemed when presented in the ringing tones of a John F. Kennedy; how gradual the process of disillusionment. Or consider the Algerian war waged by France between 1954 and 1962. Albert Camus, born in Algeria of a French father and a Spanish mother, was in many respects a typical French left-wing intellectual, yet he was never able unambiguously to take sides.

From the very beginning of the dispersion, Jews have always been faced with difficult problems of competing loyalties, liable to produce a tragic ambiguity, a double risk of failure. The tragic outcome may be deferred and may never occur during the lifetime of an individual, but when it does come, the Jew is liable to be taken pathetically unawares. The very Jew who is the proud possessor of some non-Israeli passport wakes up one morning stateless, having fondly believed himself to be thoroughly assimilated and accepted. A film by Bunuel shows some people sitting round a table, unaware that their dining-room is in fact a stage. Suddenly the curtain rises and they find themselves exposed to the audience's hostile gaze, as though surprised in the nude. The history of the Jews since the beginning of the dispersion has been full of experiences of this kind. It looks increasingly that the Jews of Argentina may be in for a similar rude awakening.

The path of self-fulfillment can be long, tortuous and difficult. "Universalism," when embraced for the right reasons, is more than an escape mechanism. Unfortunately, it has been adopted by certain Jews of the Diaspora as a pretext for refusing to face disagreeable realities and difficult personal decisions.

Thus, a French-Jewish historian, Pierre Vidal-Naquet, refers with approval to the "emergence of the remarkable 'non-Jewish Jews' who left their mark on the nineteenth and twentieth centuries,"[1] giving credit to the Jewish culture of the Diaspora (obviously, since before the creation of Israel there was no other).

There is clearly a sense in which it is easier to feel an affinity with mankind at large than to espouse a particular national cause; indeed, nationalism may be experienced as a straitjacket. To aspire to be a citizen of the world is laudable, but to invoke this aspiration as a pretext for opposing self-determination or to support the continuance of abasement and humiliation demonstrates, if not bad faith, at least a grave political shortsightedness. More especially, to imagine that Jews do not have to follow the same path to freedom as other alienated peoples is an illusion peculiar to rootless Jews. In a world divided into nations, torn between nations, to demand of the Jews alone that they be citizens of the world is to condemn them to extinction. Six million perished because they had no country to give them refuge. They were all, whether they liked it or not, stateless "universalists"—but sufficiently Jewish not to escape a very Jewish fate.

Furthermore, in varying degrees, all peoples have their community values and specific cultures, shaped by history, geography, and sometimes religion. Each member of such a community has a collective root, drawing his share of a common past from a common ground, and each people harmonizes in its own way the daily symphony of its existence. An individual without collective memories is a

---

[1]*Liaison*, Geneva, February 1971. Other quotations from this author are taken from the same source.

ghost and a stranger to the land in which by accident he was born. In the Middle Ages the Christians invented the Wandering Jew as the very symbol of apostasy, the lost soul remembering only the crime for which he was reproached. Today the anti-Zionist has difficulty grasping that the Jews have discontinued their wanderings and recovered their national past.

"You are stateless and will remain so; this is how it should be," we are told in the name of an abstract universalism. "You are as American (or as French) as your neighbour," in the name of an inconsequential assimilationism. "But," the classical anti-Semite adds, "although it is a very bad thing to be without a country, you must not expect to be as American (or as French) as the man next door." These two forces attack the Jew's sense of identity from front and rear, intent on reducing the history of Israel to nothing for the benefit of non-Jews. In the last resort, it matters little that one of these forces is generous and blind, the other clear-sighted and vicious.

I am a Jew, but I may legitimately feel more affinity for an Arab, say, than for an Irishman. But in so feeling, I shall maintain my Jewish roots, i.e., remain myself. While I may well be influenced by external factors, I cannot embrace a cause which would deny those roots or seek to destroy them. It is precisely in affirming myself as a member of the Jewish community that I am appealing to a universal human right.

Furthermore, a Jew remains a Jew whether or not he feels himself to be one. It would be in the interests of Jews to understand why. Certainly, there have been attractive "non-Jewish" Jews, first among them, perhaps, being an assimilated Jew called Theodor Herzl. But political thinking cannot be founded on personal likes or dislikes. The question is why so many Jews of the Diaspora invoke the principles of universalism.

Historically, the reason is not hard to find. Treated as less than full citizens in their countries of adoption, vaguely aware of their lack of roots, they prefer to disappear into the mass by virtue of an airy abstraction rather than to reaffirm their Jewishness, an affirmation condemned by universalism as retrograde. Thus, the leaning towards universalism is largely attributable to the Jewish feeling of rootlessness and insecurity within an alien society.

The expression "non-Jewish Jew" conjures up a mental image of a Marx or Freud. We overlook the host of the maladjusted and the neurotic who were just as much a product of the dispersion, let alone the innumerable victims of pogrom, massacre and gas chamber. And why should only those Jews whose Jewishness was least apparent be singled out for remembrance? Why should there be no recognition of those Jews who retained, demonstrated and proclaimed their Jewishness?

The Jewish socialist Ber Borochov—little known even among those Jews who claim to be socialists—was a "remarkable" man by any definition. Almost a hundred years ago he had this to say about the kind of behaviour to which the non-Zionist Jew is prone:

> What is the more surprising about our optimists: their naive enthusiasm or their stupidity? They cry progress; meanwhile, "civilized" England brutally flays the Boers to the roar of cannon and to the applause of the entire nation; "civilized" America launches a virulent campaign of racial hatred against its Negroes; Germany brandishes an arrogant militarism; the Powers are prepared to spring at each other's throats for the sake of a scrap of Turkey or China; the weak, groaning under the yoke of the strong, rob one another or flaunt their strength before those who are weaker still. . . . Is there not something less than honest in advising Jews to put all their hopes in a Progress so far from obvious?"[2]

Albert Memmi[3] reminds us that in two thousand years there have been two hundred mass expulsions of Jews from various countries, or one such expulsion, on the average, every ten years. It is all very well for the universalist to assert that the age of mass expulsions is past. We shall probably not have to wait another ten years to see him proved wrong.

Massacre as an Agent of History

The Israeli writer Claude Ranel states: "Not because we were here two thousand years ago are we entitled to be here today, but because it has taken us two thousand years to win our freedom."[4]

There is a historical, political and above all human drama behind these words, evoking as they do the victory of the authentic over the spurious. The rest—the

---

[2]"On Questions of Zionist Theory," in *Sources*, No. 2, Jerusalem, 1971.
[3]*La Libération du Juif*, Gallimard, Paris.
[4]*Moi, Juif palestinien*, Laffont, Paris.

arsenal of formulae and dates designed to belittle the drama of the Jews and to denigrate their struggle for liberation — is nothing but a stubborn attempt to distort the history of the Jewish people, to render the actors in the drama less than human, and to disparage both the sufferings of the Jews and the hopes which sustained them.

If I am turned out of hearth and home and remain outside one night, I am legally entitled to return the following day. If I suffer for ten, twenty, five thousand or fifty thousand nights, does my right of return stand in inverse relationship to the length of my exile? Quite the contrary; my right to return and recover my freedom becomes stronger in direct proportion to what I have endured, not by virtue of some abstract arithmetic, but because of the nights spent in exile, and because I want my children, and their children, to be spared a similar experience.

Moderate anti-Zionists, in their ignorance, tend to believe that Palestinian Jews are not strongly attached to the land, and extremists take good care not to dispel this ignorance, for it enables them to affirm the illegitimacy of the return to Zion. Salo W. Baron, author of an authoritative history of Israel which demonstrates the permanence of the Jewish presence in Palestine, provides some figures. Incidentally, I attach limited importance to the evidence given below for the length of Jewish history in Palestine (the reason why will shortly be explained).

Baron estimates that in the first century C.E. there were some three million Jews in Palestine, and in the seventh century, two hundred thousand. The following lines, describing the vigour of Jewish life early in the latter century, bear quotation:

> Although apparently reduced to but 10 to 15 percent of the population, Palestinian Jews were still sufficiently numerous and concentrated, especially in the northern districts, to make their weight felt in the country's affairs. Most of their thirty-one rural and twelve urban settlements recorded in that period were in Galilee. . . . Some Jews had also long defied the imperial prohibition and settled in Jerusalem. They were sufficiently numerous in the Holy City for the local governor to force them to accept baptism *en masse* in A.D. 607.[5]

Permanently present, the Jews are in almost perpetual revolt. After Massada

---

[5] Salo W. Baron, *A Social and Religious History of the Jews*, second edition, Columbia University Press, New York, 1967, Volume III, p. 20.

72 C.E.), Bar Kochba's revolt (132–135 C.E.), and the insurrection which threatened the Emperor Septimius Severus early in the third century, there was an insurrection in Galilee in the fourth century, and in the seventh a new Jewish war lasting fourteen years (614–628). This last was brought to an end by the Emperor Heraclius, who promised the insurgents an armistice in exchange for the surrender of their arms. Once they had surrendered on these terms, he went back on his promise.

These facts and figures deserve mention, for they weaken the case made for denying Israel's right to a national existence. But, as I have said, they are not in themselves decisive. Over the centuries, throughout the world, there have been innumerable migrations, conquests, and exchanges of population; new countries have been created, territory gained and lost. But the Jewish people alone, which in massacre, deportation, and forced conversion has paid the heaviest tribute of all, is somehow held responsible for its own tribulations, as if suffering were the natural fate of the Jewish people and something which, in addition, it deserves. The following is a disturbing example of this idea:

> This ancient Hebrew State, with its inadequate area, and sparsely populated, was nothing more than a tiny bit of territory to be trampled down from time to time by the mighty empires that had been rising close by, and expanding both East and West. This is a natural indication of the natural, and thereby, social process known as the struggle for existence and the survival of the fittest.[6]

Hitlerian dogma? Not at all: a declaration by His Eminence the Sheikh Nadam Al-Jisr, a Lebanese member of the Academy of Islamic Research, made at the fourth conference of that body (Cairo, September 1968). He went on to specify that "the tiny Jewish State came to an end since it had lost Divine Support which had been originally provided for the upkeep of the True Religion."[7]

Moderate anti-Zionists should take note of the remorseless logic behind this argument. Jews are guilty of wanting to resurrect a Hebrew State long since doomed to disappear by divine dispensation and the laws of history alike, and

---

[6] Fourth conference of the Academy of Islamic Research, General Organization for Government Printing Offices, Cairo, 1970. Extracts introduced and edited by D. F. Green, *Arab Theologians on Jews and Israel*, third edition, Editions de l'Avenir, Geneva, 1976, p. 49.
[7] *Ibid.*

hence should be grateful for the relative indulgence shown them by other, more favoured peoples.

Some will feel that the ways of God need no support from Darwinism. For our purposes, what is important is to keep a level head and one's feet on the ground. Frenchmen would do well to remember that most of them are not descended from the Gauls but from peoples of Germanic stock (Franks, Burgundians, Visigoths and the like). The ethnic composition of the United States is today very different from what it was in George Washington's time, a mere two hundred years ago. What concerns us is contemporary history, its problems and dramas, and the options open to its actors. What is important is not how many Jews were living in Palestine at any given moment but the huge host of those who were not, those who had to suffer for possessing no country of their own. It is because the Jews had no country that they are entitled to demand equality with those more fortunately placed. A right to national existence is not to be measured by how many people are descended from those to whom that right has been denied. The rights of others—whatever such rights may be—cannot be opposed to the right of the landless to a country of their own on the grounds that the landless are somehow condemned by fate to remain so.

The Palestinians as Our Equals

Let nobody at this point seek to weaken the argument by invoking the Palestinians. If good King Hussein, during the "Black September" of 1968, had killed off three-quarters of the Palestinians, and if the "progressive" Syrians had virtually finished off the remainder when in 1976 they marched into the Lebanon, would the remnants, scattered and leaderless, have forfeited their rights with the passage of time? Such, however, is the reasoning which anti-Zionists, even the moderates, apply to Jews. Nobody would venture to argue in this way about any other people.

Palestinian claims to self-determination have in the past been given very short shrift by the Hashemite and Baathist régimes in Jordan and Syria. Israel, on the other hand, has denied this right to the Palestinians only because it is conceived as a weapon by those who deny Israel's right to exist. Faced by a constant threat of extinction, Israel reacts in self-defence. The moderate anti-Zionists are all too fond of saying that the Israelis believe that the language of force is the only one the Palestinians understand. In fact, it is the Arab irredentists who refuse to recognize

Israel except in so far as the country has to exist to be destroyed. It is in this context that Israel is constantly being asked to pay tribute to an abstract principle by recognizing the Palestinian cause.

Let us assume that the government of Israel agrees to recognize the Palestinians in some form or other. Would this change anything?

Firstly, historical realities would remain unchanged. Israel recognized an Arab Palestine in 1948, from the very moment that Israel came into being. If ever there were two inseparable acts in history, these were they: proclamation of the existence of the State of Israel, and recognition of the other party. The importance of this point cannot be overemphasized.

While, in accordance with a United Nations decision, Israel was ratifying the creation of an Arab State in Palestine, Arab armies occupied Arab Palestine and launched an attack on that part of it which had been reserved for the Jews. Far from granting autonomy or sovereignty of any kind to those now known as the "Palestinians" (primarily among those who find the term convenient in their campaign against Israel), not one member of the Arab League, before the Six-Day War of 1967, ever called for the creation of a separate Arab Palestine, or even conceived that such a country could exist. On the contrary, any mention of "Palestinians" was condemned in the Arab world as implying the acknowledgment of frontiers imposed by colonialism on the "Arab Nation."

The PLO has trimmed its sails to suit the wind. At present, the emphasis is on the individuality of "Palestine"; in the past (although the West is less aware of this), the PLO went out of its way to link "Palestine" with Jordan, or with Jordan and the Lebanon together. The following is an extract from the "Official Report" on the eighth session of the Palestinian National Council, held in Cairo (March 1971):

> There is a natural association between Jordan and Palestine and a territorial unity shaped by history, culture and language since ancient times. The establishment of separate political entities in Palestine and Jordan is not supported by any legality nor by any constituents that form an entity. They were the product of the dismembering policy by which colonialism after World War I sought to tear asunder the unity of the Arab Nation and the Arab homeland. Nevertheless, this division could not prevent the masses east and west of the river from feeling that they were one people, faced with a plot by colonialism and Zionism.[8]

[8] Quoted by Y. Harkabi, *Palestinians and Israel*, Keter Publishing House, Jerusalem, 1974, p. 139.

More recently, the late Zoher Mossein, head of the PLO Bureau of Military Operations, said (some time before his assassination by fellow-Palestinians):

> There is no difference between Jordanians, Palestinians and Lebanese; we are all members of a single nation. Solely for political reasons are we careful to stress our identity as Palestinians, since a separate State of Palestine would be an extra weapon in Arab hands to fight Zionism with. Yes, we do call for the creation of a Palestinian State for tactical reasons. Such a State would be a new means of continuing the battle against Zionism, and for Arab unity.[9]

The only effect (even if unintentional) of the stress now being laid on the specifically Palestinian side of the Middle East conflict is to concentrate hostile attention on the Jews of Palestine. It leaves one thing unaffected, namely, that Israel, from the beginning, was the *only* Middle Eastern country to extend recognition to the Palestinian Arabs.

However, a good deal of water has flowed under the bridge since 1948. Today, Israel is expected to recognize the right to independent statehood of its sworn foes. Our moderates, who are generally pink in their outlook, find it difficult to forgive Israelis for having, in May 1977, voted into office a right-wing party with a tough line on recognition. It should not demand an overwhelming effort of imagination to understand this reaction (the majority, in fact, was not very large) in face of the stubborn hostility and ostracism to which Israel has been subjected for the past thirty years — the only harvest it has ever reaped from its recognition of an intractable enemy.

It would be well to remember, by the way, that Israel (and Jews throughout the world) has always recognized the twenty-odd Arab States which now exist. Furthermore, President Sadat's gesture — which alone of all the Arab Heads of State he was bold enough to make — has had a significant effect on Israeli public opinion.

The personality of a nation, like that of an individual, can come to fruition only through recognition of the existence of others. But what the enemies of Israel are after, in demanding recognition of an independent Palestinian State, is at the very least an act of contrition and the acceptance of enormous military risks, even the risk of complete disappearance. Here we may rely on the authority of an attentive observer: "In my view, Arafat and other Palestinians are today in favour of a

---

[9] *Trouw*, Amsterdam, March 1977.

Palestinian mini-State because they think that, in the long run, this will mean the destruction of Israel."[10] Development of a national personality? It is the PLO and the rejectionist States which are stifling their own development by refusal to recognize Israel. For that matter, the Islamic States are full of ethnic minorities whose aspirations, never recognized, are a direct cause of the crises which erupt from time to time in this part of the world.

Whether Palestinian claims are justified or not, they can be dealt with only by negotiation, which the PLO and its sympathizers consistently reject. For the time being at any rate, the main beneficiary of pro-Palestinian congresses and letters to the press is pan-Arab imperialism.

An Algerian writer, Rachid Boujedra, although the author of a book vehemently criticizing Islamic society, has devoted another to explaining that the sufferings of the Palestinians derive entirely from Jewish expansionism, itself fed by religious bigotry, and describes how "the State of Israel has been permitted gradually to encroach on its neighbours, in accordance with Old Testament precept. . . . Herzl's theories have emptied Palestine of its inhabitants and brought in Jews from all over the world, thus giving effect to the prophecies of Joshua."[11]

This same author was moved to pity when passing a miserable Kurdish refugee camp, yet never asks himself who is responsible for these people's fate. Such narrowness of outlook, such incapacity even to conceive that there might be another view (Israeli or Kurdish), is unfortunately typical of much Arab (and contemporary Iranian) thinking. Barring revolution—which Sadat's gesture may herald or help to bring about—this is likely to prevent the Arabs and Iranians from tackling their own pressing domestic problems effectively.

It is surprising that some left-wing writers should show so little understanding of the fact that anti-Zionism has as one of its objectives to divert, and harness for its own purposes, any revolutionary stirrings in the Middle East. Political speculation in this part of the world is largely vitiated by an obstinate refusal to face facts, as witness, for instance, the barrenness of a stance which, while totally ignoring Israel, claims to be right and just by definition and yet calls on the "international community" for approval.

I do not reject the other party and should like nothing so much as to bring them

---

[10]Interview with Colonel Qaddafi, *La Stampa*, 21 November 1976.
[11]*La Répudiation*, Denoël, Paris, and *Journal palestinien*, Hachette, Paris.

to the conference table. I am anxious that the files should be opened and all relevant problems examined. I am not afraid of any witness who may be called, and I recognize in advance, as anybody in good faith must, that the other party is entitled to prove that they have suffered injury and to claim compensation. This does not mean, however, that I accept in advance the justice of the charges brought against me, nor that I will abstain from putting forward my own claims for damages. Above all, I cannot agree to being condemned in advance, and *in absentia*. How long will moderate anti-Zionists continue to follow the lead of extremists for whom the scales of justice are already dipped?

Talk of mutual recognition tends to mask the fact that recognition of Israel by the PLO, and that of the PLO by Israel, are two very different things, with different connotations for the parties concerned. Recognition of Israel would put Palestinian nationalism on the same footing as all authentic liberation movements. At the height of the Franco-Algerian war, the Algerian independence movement never dreamed of destroying France; nor has the IRA, for all the wrongs done to Ireland in the course of history, called for the destruction of England. Recognition of the PLO by Israel, as things are at present, would demand that Israel recognize its own nonexistence. As long as the PLO refuses to admit the existence of Israel, any demands, objurgations, winks, or nudges designed to force Israel to recognize the PLO, far from serving the cause of peace, serve the interests of one side only.

This is not to say that successive Israeli governments, including Menahem Begin's, have been, and always are, right. While refusal to take suicidal risks with national security is understandable, it is still legitimate to regret a certain rigidity, an inadequate awareness of Palestinian realities and of the way in which international sympathies have been enlisted in the Arab cause. Furthermore, certain statements by Israeli spokesmen have been, to put it mildly, inopportune. However, these are venial shortcomings. Lack of diplomatic tact is perhaps inevitable in a young and vigorous democracy (and Israel is the only democracy, be it remembered, in the Middle East).

What would be implied by PLO recognition of Israel? At best, realistic negotiations instead of blind destruction, and a willingness to drop absurd, though superficially plausible, claims, such as that Israel should become a "secular, democratic State"—as though politicians who have no idea of what democracy implies (this is no reproach but a statement of fact) could or should impose on Israel a form of government traditionally repugnant to Islam.

We are still far from these minimal changes. In the meantime, Palestinian spokesmen seem to accept without difficulty the continued persecution of Jews in Syria, Iraq, and the Soviet Union. They honour the memory of King Feisal of Saudi Arabia, a narrow, reactionary fanatic, anti-Jewish in every fibre of his being, and have hurried to the defence of Khomeini, who in this respect is little better than Feisal. They are full of gratuitous references to the Palestinian Charter, with its shrill call for elimination of the "Zionist entity" (implying the physical destruction of the Israeli nation). The Political and Organizational Programme adopted in Damascus in January 1979 by the fourteenth session of the Palestinian Council[12] intransigently reaffirms the principles of the Charter and goes on to say: "The PLO affirms the importance of alliance with the socialist countries, and first and foremost, with the Soviet Union."

The position is complicated, but the choice facing Israel is simple, as always when a nation's existence is at stake. In the short run, as long as the enemy pursues his ends by criminal means, he will be pursued as a criminal; in the long run, as soon as he renounces these means, all sorts of doors will be found open.

The government of Israel may be criticized for not having sufficiently explored the ground with this in view. It seems to have been caught unawares now that negotiations with Egypt have begun. This is not, however, wickedness, but simply a lack of political judgment. In this connection, it is not irrelevant to recall that European resistance movements during the Second World War did not try to decide in advance what settlement should be imposed on Germany, engrossed as they were—and as Israel is today—in battle against an implacable foe.

However iniquitous the Treaty of Versailles may have been, mitigating circumstances have never been recognized with respect to the crimes committed by the Third Reich. Nor has anybody claimed that such crimes were cancelled out by the ruthlessness of Allied bombing attacks on German cities. The crimes committed in the name of "Free Palestine" are alone, it seems, in being viewed with understanding and justified in advance whenever Israel, goaded beyond endurance by some outrage, resorts to a legitimate act of self-defence. A French popular magazine, not especially noted for its sympathy with Third World aspirations, ventures to find mitigating circumstances for the failure of the Syrians to abide by the conventions (ratified by them) concerning the protection of prisoners of war, on the grounds that creation of the State of Israel had "caused a prejudice to

---

[12]*Journal of Palestine Studies*, Beirut, 1979, 3, p. 166.

the Arab countries in all sorts of ways"[13] and created understandable resentment. Privileged victims (but why them and not, say, the Tibetans?), the Palestinians are thus promoted to the ranks of privileged killers (and why should the Angolan UNITA movement not be accorded this privilege too?).

PLO outrages had to be atrocious indeed before a French university lecturer (who introduced himself in a letter to a French weekly as "hostile to Zionism") could condemn them as "racism and anti-Semitism triumphant, closing the door to all but war or genocide."[14] Atrocious indeed they had to be before this moderate anti-Zionist had to confess to being "sick with nausea and anguish." Israelis, who have more direct, ancient and lasting reasons for nausea and anguish, cannot afford not to keep a clear head.

This being so, it is mockery to maintain that right being exclusively on the side of the Palestinians, there is no limit to what they may legitimately do. I would prefer to recognize them as authentic human beings, devoid of their sinister trappings. Toleration carried beyond certain limits is a humiliation of those to whom it is extended and a poor service rendered to the Palestinians by their self-styled friends.

The Palestinians have not yet been able freely to express their views as to who should represent them, and no group, simply because it makes more noise than any other and takes a heavier toll of human life, can claim to be their exclusive representative. Furthermore, the PLO has itself been overtaken by the violence for which it set the fashion. At Tunis Airport, November 1974, and at Orly (Paris), January 1975, other *fedayeen* shouted down the PLO representatives and threatened their lives. Terrorism leads to super-terrorism, and the protectors of terrorists may be hoist with their own petard, as happened to the unfortunate representatives of OPEC countries attending a ministerial meeting in Vienna (December 1975).

The "progressive" friends of the *fedayeen* project on to the PLO their own frustrated aspirations to social revolution and their own warped ideas of justice. They might at least ask themselves: How is it that the Palestinian guerrilla fighters, unwilling to take on Israeli troops, are reduced to the murder of children? Why is it that Palestinian official communiqués command no credence, even among the *fedayeen* themselves? Why is it that their declared aim—the destruction of

[13]*Paris-Match*, Paris, 19 January 1974.
[14]Letter from Yves Parson to Jean Daniel, in *Le Nouvel Observateur*, Paris, 2–8 December 1974.

Israel—is not only as far off as ever, but no longer appears in the official catalogue of claims made by the Arab countries? Why had President Sadat, far more lucid and aware of the true interests of the Arab peoples, so bravely swum against the tide (followed by the bulk of Egyptian public opinion)?

These questions are put to moderate anti-Zionists who, while unable to applaud the slaughter of children, consider themselves politically sophisticated. Have they ever attempted to see the problem in political terms? Probably not, and for one essential reason: "Zionism" for them has sinister connotations, and hides the living realities of the people of Israel. Yet surely those who do not share the blindness of the extreme anti-Zionists should be able to understand that Israelis, too, can display courage, patriotism and maturity of judgment, and that the Israeli nation is made up of real people, not of rapacious settlers with hooked fingers, sucking the life-blood of their unfortunate victims.

Those who claim to be helping in the emergence of a Palestinian entity by supporting the PLO are defending a cause which can offer nothing but destruction, of itself as well as of others. They are encouraging it in the pursuit of its illusions. What I refuse to recognize is not a living Palestinian reality, but a movement which claims to speak on their behalf yet takes so exclusively negative a stance. And I decline to believe that the Palestinians can be represented only by demagogues and butchers, who deny the existence of one party to the detriment of both. One day, I trust, we shall see the birth of a representative movement which will be prepared to exist, on an equal footing, with Israel, recognizing the Jews of Israel for what they are, without aspiring to eliminate them by destruction or absorption, or by emasculation of all that Israel stands for.

A *False Symmetry*

The PLO and its branches reject every issue other than the elimination of Israel—not without a certain hypocrisy, as when their leaders refer merely to the "legitimate rights of the Palestinian people." As to how this should be interpreted, moderate anti-Zionists with no taste for blood and not particularly anxious to set the Palestinians off on a path which can but lead to a general conflagration (in which the Palestinian Arabs would be the first to suffer) maintain an embarrassed silence or get lost in inessentials. For the one and only aim pursued by the PLO is to set Arabs and Jews at each other's throats. Why cannot moderate anti-Zionists (especially when Jews) unequivocally condemn murderous folly as an instrument of policy?

The answer is perhaps to be found in the following lines, written at the beginning of the century by yet another Zionist socialist, Nahman Syrkin:

> Impelled by their Judaism towards Revolution, the socialists erred in that they did not guard the purity of their revolt. Instead of emphasizing their kinship with an oppressed people, in their revolutionary opposition to the class society, instead of protesting first of all as Jews and then broadening their attitude to give it a universal application, they did just the opposite.[15]

The moderate Jewish anti-Zionists, as well, believe that the surest way to prevent terrorism is for Israel to yield ground in the hope of gaining acceptance. They underrate the determination of Israel's enemies and show little understanding of what Israel stands for. Do they really believe that the adolescent refugee from North Africa, in Kiryat Shemona or Safed, whose brother or sister has just been the victim of hysterical Arab violence, will decide that he ought to yield on the grounds that the perpetrators of such violence are somehow more entitled to life than he is?

Israel is a living, organized community, and reacts in self-defence like any other. Israelis are not, as a grotesque propaganda would like to depict them, a conglomeration of shadows lurking in some limbo, torn between fear and the impulse to aggression; they are not, as one author puts it, in words which in their wholesale dismissal of everything Israel represents could hardly be improved on by the most rabid Jew-hater, "obscure stateless persons from nobody knows where."[16] It is frightening that certain Jews of the Diaspora should react to the contempt felt for them by draping themselves in a spurious universalist generosity. Their doubts and self-questionings are sterile, encouraging resignation—weapons they have laboriously forged against themselves.

Confronted with violence on the one hand, misunderstanding on the other, the Israelis are alone entitled to judge how effective is their way of fighting a battle imposed on them. As one Israeli author has written: "The Arabs may fight against Israel and do her harm, but if Israel fights back she is aggressive."[17] The inexplicable behaviour of certain Jews, to which Syrkin refers, cannot be understood unless

---
[15]"Internationalism v. Nationalism," in *Sources*, Jerusalem, No. 2, 1971.
[16]A. Zayed, *El Moudjahid*, Algiers, 15 May 1974.
[17]Y. Harkabi, *op. cit.*, p. 16.

it is realized that this one-sidedness has infected all anti-Zionist thinking, even that of the moderates. The phenomenon is insufficiently explained by the power of the propaganda put out by the oil-producing countries or by the enormous economic leverage they exert; masochism comes into it as well. There is a precedent in the number of people who espoused National Socialism in countries where its beliefs would seem to have corresponded to no historically explicable need.

The friends of the PLO establish a false moral symmetry between attempts to destroy a community and the reprisals that community must resort to in self-defence. Since a virtual state of war exists between Israeli and Arab secret services, it is absurd for a Jew to feign indignation at the death in action of an Israeli agent. The other side, however, exercises no such restraint. In January 1973, a PLO official, Mahmood El-Hamshari, came to a violent and mysterious end in Paris; Golda Meir, visiting that city some time later, was greeted with shouts of "Nazi!" by left-wing demonstrators protesting against this assassination. The world had to wait for more than five years before learning that "a Palestinian volunteer, one Salim Hussein, has been shot in a Lebanese *fedayeen* camp for high treason. The charge, brought by Palestinian leaders, was that he had been a party to the attack on Mahmood El–Hamshari, believed to have favoured compromise."[18] Incidentally, it is not easy to see why a man who, not being himself in the firing line, organizes killings at one remove, should expect personal immunity.

Reprisals are a means (questionable and perhaps ineffective; there is constant argument on this matter in Israel itself) of attacking the camps where the *fedayeen* are trained for murderous and indiscriminate assault on Israeli civilians. Israel has never bombed the innocent for the fun of it, nor, for that matter, sought to play James Bond, as at Entebbe. Israelis see these raids as acts of perfectly legitimate self-defence, from which no other country in a similar position would abstain. They have a deep-seated fear, a product of their own history, of indiscriminate massacre; rejectionist hysteria, and the absence of international reaction to it, do nothing to reassure them. Are such fears shared by Arab refugees and civilians? Historically speaking, there is no reason why they should be; there have never been unpopular, powerless Arab minorities living under the shadow of destruction. The Arabs are, of course, constantly being told that "they cannot help but dream of destroying Israel"[19] by persons who would be better employed in persuading them

---

[18]*France-Soir*, Paris 7–8 May 1978.
[19]As put by Maxime Rodinson, see Chapter IV.

of something which the moderate anti-Zionists, even the communists, say they recognize, namely, the legitimacy and the reality of the State of Israel.

As to the Palestinian camps, every effort is made to create confusion in the public mind between "refugee camp," with its connotation of women and children huddled together in discomfort, and the *fedayeen* training centres. The *fedayeen* themselves are depicted against a different background. In their camouflaged uniforms, against a rising sun, manfully standing with guns at the ready (guns which have more than once been used against sleeping children, a fact it is fashionable to overlook), these youths become "freedom fighters." Care is taken not to show them photographed against battered walls or surrounded by mangled bodies—scenes familiar enough in other contexts, except that killings of Biafrans in Nigeria, of Lebanese by Syrians, of Kurds by Iraqis and Iranians, have been far more systematic and murderous. It is no accident that training takes place in areas where there are heavy concentrations of displaced persons, since any Israeli counterattack is almost bound to cause suffering to noncombatants. Photographs of the destruction wrought make excellent propaganda material, as the Germans discovered in disseminating pictures showing the effects of Allied air raids on Hamburg and the Ruhr. At a camp in Jordan, Jean Genêt[20] talked with a woman "who quietly but firmly corrected me when I spoke of refugee camps. 'You mean military camps; everybody's armed and trained for battle now.' " The four young Palestinians responsible for the hijacking which began in Palma (Majorca) and ended in sanguinary circumstances at Mogadiscio (October 1977) had been trained in a camp of this kind. When in July and August 1976 Arab forces laid siege to Tel-el-Zaatar in the Lebanon (a combined refugee camp-cum-military training centre), leaving thousands of sick and wounded without water or attention, the PLO reaped the poisoned fruit of a policy impoverished, because unbalanced, by the weight of its venomous hatred of Israel.

Nor is it an accident that of the world's innumerable refugees, the Palestinians alone escape the attentions of the United Nations High Commissioner for Refugees. As a result, they have vegetated in camps for years, instead of being absorbed by the host countries, as has happened everywhere else. In India, in Black Africa, in Western Germany, since the end of the Second World War, some twenty million persons have been resettled. In January 1972, in the Kermanshah area

---

[20]French writer, ex-convict, a champion of the Baader-Meinhof gang and an apologist for political violence. (*Le Monde diplomatique*, Paris, July 1974.)

(Iranian Kurdistan) I visited a refugee camp whose inmates had been expelled overnight, in their thousands, from Iraq, merely because they were of Iranian origin. On inquiring in Teheran as to how long they were expected to remain there, I was told that their absorption would "take some time." "How long will that be?" "Oh, perhaps a couple of weeks."

Many people, Israelis and pro-Israelis, are shocked by reprisals and vocal in airing their indignation. In the opposite camp, there is silence, even jubilation, when the victims are Jewish civilians. After the slaughter at Maalot in May 1974, an official statement by the Franco-Arab Solidarity Association declared that Israel had forced the Arabs into such action, adding as an afterthought that the taking of hostages was of course to be condemned. This attitude is reminiscent of that adopted by Parisian collaborators, who in 1943, while supporting the policies of the Third Reich, were prepared to admit, in passing, that it was none too pleasant to be a Jew at that time. Today, the Jews who have resurrected a nation, and especially those who survived massacre under the Third Reich, have decided that never again shall there be such a thing as a death camp. Such determination seems to cause consternation in certain quarters. Those in the West who are constantly wondering whether Israel is justified in existing should ask themselves whether their attitude, by inducing Israelis to feel that they can count only on themselves, does not in fact help to produce reprisals which are bound to shock the soft, the safe, and the well-to-do.

Similar things occurred in the Second World War. But to deplore the ruthlessness of the bombing of Dresden in March 1945, when the Reich was visibly crumbling, is not to question whether the Allies were right in opposing Hitler. Does it follow that because these raids were cruel, the Nazis were somehow right or that we should at least suspend judgment? Yet this is how people all too often reason about Israel and the Arabs. Incidentally, it is difficult to see what benefit "Franco-Arab solidarity" derives from reasoning of this sort.

Israel is fighting a battle for survival. It must fight or go under. The PLO can choose between further murderous assaults and the negotiated settlement which in recent years has become the rule between civilized nations. The PLO aspires to destroy Israel, but Israel has no ambition to destroy any Arab State. To put both camps on the same footing, as the moderate anti-Zionists do, is to see a symmetry where none exists.

In another respect, a kind of symmetry does obtain, although Israel's detractors constantly overlook it. Jewish refugees from Arab countries have had to cope with the same sort of problems as those faced by Arab refugees from Israel: hardship, difficulties of adaptation, questions of compensation. It is true that the majority of the Jews in question (not without grave difficulty on occasion) have been absorbed as citizens of Israel, while the Arabs remain quartered in camps deliberately maintained to perpetuate resentment and ensure a supply of cannon-fodder. It is not irrelevant to mention the Greco-Turkish War which ended in 1923. A million Greek refugees from Turkey were resettled in Greece, and Turks in large numbers re-absorbed in Turkey, after which the problem ceased to exist.

A Preliminary Look at Russian Colonialism

Many moderate anti-Zionists, generous though not particularly clear-headed, have developed a delicate sense of justice when balancing Arab against Jew. The following is the kind of charge liable to be brought against us: "You, and many Jews like you, seem to think that only Jews exist."[21]

The position, as Zionists see it, is quite the opposite. They see a general tendency to deny to Jews, and to Jews alone, the freedom to declare oneself a member of, and to belong to, a distinctive community if one so desires, and to share in the defence of that community. To wish to be Jewish is to claim no privilege and to assert no superiority; it is simply to demand rights that other peoples enjoy.

P. Vidal-Naquet writes as follows to bolster his charge of egoism: "I learn from the press that a non-Jewish Lithuanian has just been condemned to death by a Soviet court for hijacking an aircraft. Why has there been no protest from the Jewish community?"[22]

The plain fact is that Jews have often been strongly represented in national liberation movements and demonstrations of solidarity. Today, for instance, Jews are playing no small part in left-wing movements hostile to Israel. This is a drama almost peculiar to the Jews, and there are historical reasons to explain it; Vidal-Naquet, and others like him, in failing to perceive this, themselves reveal a typically Jewish complex. The classical charge brought against Jews by nationalistically minded anti-Semites (including Stalin) is that they lack national loyalties.

[21] P. Vidal-Naquet, ibid.
[22] *Ibid.*

The left-wing anti-Semite of today, on the other hand, accuses them of being blinded to the interests of others by Jewish national feelings. Yet nobody expects an Irishman to take up the cudgels on behalf of Quebec or Corsica. Nobody, as far as I am aware, expects an Arab to go out of his way to proclaim his solidarity with the Czechoslovaks. Although, be it observed in parenthesis, one would at least like the Arabs not to gloat over the sufferings of others, as the leaders and press of almost all the Arab countries did on the occasion of the Soviet invasion of Czechoslovakia in 1968. Moreover, the Algerian paper *El Moudjahid* was perhaps the only journal in the world, outside the Soviet Union, to express open satisfaction at the death sentence passed on two Leningrad Jews (December 1970) and, before that sentence was commuted, to demand their heads.

The accusation of ethnic egoism, as being a fault peculiar to Jews, is therefore singularly hard to sustain. But for the sake of accuracy, and because the enemies of Israel suffer from occasional amnesia, the following points should be made.

Firstly, a specifically Jewish problem does exist, and Jewish activists in the Soviet Union are facing up to it with a carefully considered programme of political action. What they must at all costs avoid is a charge of overt anti-Sovietism. They have therefore decided against a head-on attack, and hence to concern themselves only with matters of immediate relevance to them as Soviet Jews. They make one basic claim, which is to be allowed to live on an equal footing with all the other multifarious nationalities of the Soviet Union. Should the Kremlin not allow this, for tactical or ideological reasons (and Marxist theory is particularly muddled about the Jewish problem), they claim the right to national self-determination. Jewish communities in the West fully understand the reasons for this attitude, realizing that effective action depends on the maintenance of a low profile. They know that Jews would be the first to suffer if the Kremlin's overall policies were to be overtly challenged.

The fact remains that, according to those who have managed to leave the Soviet Union, Jews in prisons and psychiatric wards are still demonstrating support for the Lithuanians and other Soviet minorities.[23] During the Soviet invasion of Czechoslovakia in August 1968, the only demonstrators with the courage to face beatings and imprisonment by assembling in Red Square were a handful of Jews. In thus displaying solidarity with the Czechoslovaks, they were in no way forgoing their specific claims as Jews. In similar fashion, the resistance movements, both

[23] Y. Sevela, in *L'Express*, Paris, 28 June—4 July 1971.

Christian and communist, under the Third Reich had encouraged a common resistance by making their own specific contributions and not by submerging themselves in the mass. Solidarity in suffering is more likely to result from a pooling of individual experiences than from a willingness on the part of any one group to suppress its individuality for the benefit of others.

Left-wing intellectuals are reticent with regard to Israel and quick to criticize it for its sins of commission and omission. They are strangely silent about the oppression endured by the Baltic countries ever since their annexation by the Soviet Union in June 1940. Why do they not demand that former Stalinists make an act of contrition for having approved that annexation, with its sequel of mass deportations and police rule?

This is a particular instance of a general rule: anything Jews may do or not do is liable to cause virtuous indignation, which in turn can be blown up into a pretext for persecution. What is distressing is that with the emancipation of the Jews of the Diaspora, the anti-Semites should have been able to recruit so many tortured spirits from the ranks of the Jews themselves.

Thus Pierre Vidal-Naquet laments the passing of a time when "so many Jews understood that their own salvation was to be achieved only through the salvation of all." Unfortunately, there never was a time when Jews *understood* anything of the sort. At the most, the Jews he admires *hoped* for assimilation in the countries where they happened to be, pending such time as frontiers should cease to exist. This has always been an aspiration of certain Jews, despite the grim lessons of history.

I look at the matter the other way around. Freedom (the term "salvation" has an eschatological ring) for all, and for the Palestinian Arabs in particular, will be brought about by the deliverance of the Jews. Not, again, that the Jews have any special claim to privilege, but because the attitude adopted towards them by others serves as a touchstone. An anti-Semitic government discredits itself in all its doings. A society which discourages its anti-Semites is better equipped to deal with its various other problems. Once the Soviet leaders cease to condemn Israel root and branch and in all its doings, once Israel is no longer the permanent defendant in a court formed by those least qualified to sit in judgment, a great step forward will have been taken towards freedom for all, including the numerous other ethnic minorities in the Soviet Union—a fact well understood in the Kremlin.

Until then, it should suffice to see the Jewish problem in strictly human terms.

The aim—and the progress made, if it is achieved, will be enormous—is simply to ensure that a people is no longer deprived of national self-expression.

Dispersion has warped the vision of many Jews. They fail to see that only by working for their own national liberation will they join the mainstream of the forces now working for greater freedom in society at large. The new awareness displayed by the Soviet Jews is an example for democrats and opponents in the Soviet world. The peoples colonized by Moscow, the deported Moslem Tartars of the Crimea, the occupied Czechs, the annexed Lithuanians, are perfectly aware of this. Dreaming as they do of throwing off the yoke of a Russian police state, they see in the attitude of Soviet Jewry a model for revolutionary action. The conclusion must be that oppressed minorities can achieve true universalism only by affirming their own personalities and not by attempting to deny them.

III
Anti-Zionists and Jews in the Other Camp: Extremists or Pro-Palestinians

The distinction between moderate and extreme anti-Zionists, although useful, does not cover the world of shifting, often incoherent opinion (the incoherence being, if anything, more marked among the anti-Zionists of Jewish origin) between the two poles.

The extremist is closed to human problems, unable to grasp their spirit or the dialectic which governs them. He prefers an absolute view, before which everything must yield, even life itself. The theorists of fascism and Stalinism provide good examples of this attitude. Though not all extreme anti-Zionists can be accused of a residual loyalty to, or leanings toward, totalitarianism, they all favour swift authoritarian action to settle complicated human problems. (Fascism had little else to offer; Stalinism did at least pay lip-service to humanitarian ideals.) These people are not always proud of their past views and would sometimes prefer them to be forgotten, although this does not erase their responsibilities for the past and, if anything, complicates the mental gymnastics required to find new ground.

The Latest Avatar of Anti-Judaism

The extreme anti-Zionist categorically refuses to recognize the Jews as a people or Israel as a nation. There is nothing in history on which the Jews could base a claim to nationhood. Furthermore, the extreme anti-Zionist invokes moral grounds; such a claim, were it to be made, would be evil. Zion, in so far as it exists, ought to be dismantled. In so far as a Jewish problem does exist at all, it will disappear only through assimilation.

Extreme anti-Zionism, curiously enough, is often professed by those of left-wing views who in other contexts readily support national liberation movements. The cause of Jewish nationalism alone is never allowed to carry any weight, and certainly not if its assertion should thwart in any way the claims to nationhood—however questionable—of some other ethnic group. It is as if the natural rights of the people of Quebec were always to be subordinated to the interests of the English-speaking majority of Canada. In substance if not in form, this anti-Zionism is of the reactionary kind popular in Arab countries of the rejectionist camp, where Sadat is howled down as a traitor, Judaism and Zionism are blithely confused, and Islamic pan-Arabism alone is allowed to mete out the law (justly triumphant in victory, the victim of grave injustice and humiliation in defeat, the only party present at the Tribunal of History, where it is at one and the same time judge, prosecuting attorney and jury, Israel being the perpetual defendant). Like classical anti-Semites, extreme anti-Zionists are not incapable of a dispassionate appraisal of world history, but all objectivity vanishes when the Jews appear upon the scene. That any specifically Jewish problem exists is denied. Jewish aspirations to nationhood, whenever emerging in the course of history, have been very properly ignored or suppressed. Peoples whose interests have brought them into conflict with the Jews are exalted, and the only part the Jews may play is a passive one.

In the Israeli-Palestinian conflict, the Palestinians are the moral victors, not so much because everybody loves an Arab as because the Arabs deny (and are encouraged by the anti-Zionists to deny) the human and political rights to which the Jews aspire.

Many of the attacks launched on the State of Israel in recent years have been characterized by an almost unparalleled malice. In its extreme form anti-Zionism is a fashionable avatar of anti-Semitism—the outward and visible sign of a deep-seated, often unconscious prejudice and spite allied to that urge to dominate others which is today castigated as being the worst impulse behind imperialism.

Zionism is the national freedom movement of the Jewish people. No less a person than Andrei Gromyko, Foreign Minister of the Soviet Union, first described it as such. On 21 May 1948, in the United Nations Security Council, he expressed his government's "surprise at the position adopted by the Arab States on the Palestine Question, and particularly at the fact that these States—or some of them, at least—are sending their troops into Palestine and carrying out military operations aimed at the suppression of the national liberation movement in Palestine."[1] Furthermore, the whole history of the Jewish people abundantly proves that the creation of a Jewish national State is the only sure way of defending the freedom and dignity of Jews and even their lives. Precarious "golden ages" and respites which the Jews have from time to time enjoyed in the course of history do not invalidate this assertion.

The anti-Zionist becomes an overt anti-Semite as soon as he goes beyond criticism of the policies of the Jerusalem government (a favourite activity of the Israelis themselves) and challenges the very existence of the State of Israel. For to refuse the Jews their right to nationhood is to perpetuate their bondage. To "de-Zionize" Israel would be like trying to "de-Helvetize" Switzerland. The fact that Israel has an Arab minority is shocking only to those for whom the idea of a Jewish majority in any country is intolerable. Yugoslavia (to say nothing of the newly independent African countries) is a mosaic, comprising, besides the Slavs—themselves divided into several groups with a long history of disunity—Albanian, Roumanian, German, Hungarian, Italian and other minorities, yet nobody questions its legitimacy. The Lebanon is another artificial creation dating from the end of the First World War; the Western Powers are significantly fond of proclaiming the importance they attach to its "territorial integrity."

There is another point which sometimes passes unperceived. Judaism (or Israel) is an ethno-religious complex. Father Marcel Dubois, a Dominican living in Jerusalem, explains this well:

> The fundamental point to grasp is the link, in the Jewish-Israeli sense of identity, between nationhood and religion. It is not enough to say that Israel is a synthesis of religion and nation, for the unity goes even deeper. Religion and nation are identified; a people with a religious vocation; a religion embodied in the nation.
>
> This intimate link between religion and nation, as part of the Jewish sense of identity, remains discernable throughout the ages, and is apparent today in the attachment of Israelis to their country. To affirm that this

[1] United Nations, Security Council, Third Year, No. 71, 299th Meeting, Official Records, 21 May 1948.

close union necessarily leads to a theocracy, however, is a mistake made only by those who view Judaism and Israel from the outside.[2]

It might be added that the secular State, a luxury which Catholics (for instance) can today recognize without recanting their faith, is a phenomenon of very recent appearance in the Christian West, where for centuries a church separate from the secular power was unimaginable, or at most an idea entertained by minorities for their own political ends. Even today, this change in outlook has not spread to the Eastern churches. A secular Islam, too, is a contradiction in terms; in the Middle East, the idea of a secular State is merely a weapon recently added to the armoury of the PLO. Turkey, of course, likes to consider itself a European country on the strength of reforms dictated by Ataturk's personal dislike of Islam, but even here nobody can be quite sure what the future holds. The Arabs know full well that their brethren, whether Moslem or Christian, cannot accept the idea because they have never learned to live together (as witness the bloodshed which has been proceeding, on and off, in the Lebanon since 1975).

Those in the West (and they are especially numerous in France) for whom religion, or membership of a religious confession, plays little or no part in their sense of identity sometimes talk as though the only common link which Jews can legitimately claim is that provided by the synagogue. This is just one prong in the attack on the Jewish sense of identity, which represents an indissoluble ethno-religious whole. In present circumstances, a secular Jewish State would be a body without a soul; the Jews restricted to their synagogues, a soul without a body.

History is unpredictable. The Israelis might one day decide to be Jews no longer (or Jewish in some other way); the Libyans might be converted to Buddhism; the French (to judge by the interest displayed—especially since the oil crisis—by influential circles in everything to do with Islam) to the religion of the Prophet. But such things are not going to happen tomorrow. All one can hope is that, should they come about, they will be the result of decisions freely taken by the countries and peoples concerned. But extreme anti-Zionism is totalitarian, wishing to impose on Israel an unwanted "democracy" which would be no more than a cover for domination by one of the two parties to the conflict.

---

[2]*Rencontres*, Jerusalem, August 1970.

"The Most Dangerous Sequel of Cannibalism" (J. V. Stalin)

On the other hand, it is comforting to read the following statement, made at a time when a brief respite had been allowed in a country where anti-Zionism had long been part of official policy:

> Although Stalin said that anti-Semitism was the most dangerous sequel of cannibalism, his name will remain associated with an absurd variety of anti-Semitism born in certain socialist countries under the new name of anti-Zionism . . . a sad, ridiculous, reactionary, and very dangerous phenomenon.[3]

The Stalin era showed that there was no need to taste human flesh to deal in terror; all that was necessary was that heads should be made to roll. For Hitler, such heads were Jewish. If he had (or thought he had) incinerated the last Jew, he would probably have begun looking round for non-Jews to play the same part. George Orwell, in *1984*, describes the absolute dictator's urge to provide a scapegoat in the form of an opposition which can be depicted as a many-headed hydra, incessantly reemerging so that it may again be put down. "Let the demons and those who worship them be forever destroyed and confounded!" exclaims the chorus in Racine's *Esther*. It would seem, however, that both cannot be true at the same time; if destroyed, the demons cannot be confounded. Those who go out of their way to invent demons sometimes overlook this.

Today, when the future of two peoples, an entire region, perhaps the world, hangs in the balance, the extreme anti-Zionists continue to interpret Israel's every action as a dual affront to their deepest convictions: anything Israel may do reveals the existence of an entity which for them does not exist; on the other hand, this non-entity is the incarnate symbol of unfathomable evil. Darquier de Pellepoix, a Vichy Commissioner for Jewish Affairs during the Second World War, was in a similar uncomfortable position, denying that Jews were being massacred yet saying that their destruction was highly desirable.

There is plenty of violently anti-Jewish writing to choose from today; it makes painful, sometimes unintentionally comic, reading. I shall offer a few examples

---

[3]*Reporter*, Prague, March 1969. Note the date; this publication, the official organ of the Union of Czechoslovak Journalists, was still (to its cost) faithful to the milder line inaugurated in January 1968, before the Soviet invasion.

only, beginning with a case of hatred for the Jews which the author of the words quoted would prefer to hide, and going on to a case in which unconscious prejudice joins forces with an untroubled conscience to resurrect the ancient charge of "ritual murder." I shall show that the concept of original sin and the legend of the Wandering Jew are still not dead. I shall discuss the extremes to which Christian anti-Zionism can go. And last but not least, my theme will be Jewish anti-Zionism; Moslem anti-Zionism will be considered in the next chapter.

Neo-Anti-Semitic Hatred

A communist daily paper published in Switzerland[4] adds a murderous touch to its hatred of Israelis, although camouflaged in revolutionary terminology. The phenomenon is the more interesting in that overt incitement to terrorism is rare in the communist press. The author is talking about the *fedayeen*:

> In open war against Israel they have proved inept, but this worries them little. Being aware of their ineptitude, they resort to terrorism, the weapon of the poor and the oppressed who have nothing but their lives—and the lives of others—to sacrifice.

The author of this quotation probably never imagined that the time would not be far distant when the kind of struggle he favoured (providing it be directed exclusively against Israel) would be resorted to by an authentically "poor and oppressed" people, namely, the Afghans. Their example may well be noticed and imitated by other, genuinely exploited peoples in Asia, the Caucasus and Eastern Europe, at present suffering under Russian imperialism. In the meantime, the western Stalinist press still takes its cue from Moscow, although it does not, as the Kremlin does, try to justify the pogroms of a former age.[5]

There is no need to be a communist to be an anti-Semite. Professor Vincent Monteil, a French historian of Islamic institutions and a Gaullist, writes that "Jews exasperate their best friends and would try the patience of angels." He inquires:

---

[4]*Voix ouvrière*, organ of the Swiss Labour (communist) Party, Geneva, 8 September 1970.
[5]See Chapter IV, under "The Right Kind of Jew and the Horrid Zionists."

Will nobody publicly acknowledge, with me, that we are sick and tired of being blackmailed by all this talk of Hitlerian persecution? Do the Gypsies pass their time rubbing our noses in Camp Dora? It is absolutely true that as soon as they find themselves in a position of strength, the jews[6] become sure of themselves and overbearing.[7]

Monteil is pleased with his comparison; we find it also in a lecture delivered at Dakar (Senegal) on 22 November 1967:

In the first place, jews were not unique in being deported. Germaine Tillon and Geneviève de Gaulle were deported too. Nor were they unique in being exterminated; millions of Gypsies, entire tribes, went to the gas chambers. We hear no talk of a "Gypsy National Home." But then there is no Gypsy Rothschild.

An overbearing Jew myself, I would readily rub Monteil's nose in the sufferings of the Gypsies, which are likely to continue until they can produce their own Herzl or Ben-Gurion. As to the two French ladies he mentions, they were warmly welcomed home, whereas the stateless Jews on the *Exodus* were refused permission to land and shipped back to the camps from which they had just been released. The only possible lesson to be drawn from these two very different fates is that the Jews, like other minorities, ought to have a national home.

Professor Monteil goes so far as to compare the fate of elderly innocent Jews hanged in Baghdad by a savage government with that of the German war criminals executed at Nuremberg: "At that time," he writes, "we gave spies short shrift."[8] These remarks on the hangings ordered by Nazam Kazzar, Chief of the Iraqi security services (executed in his turn in 1973), should be read in conjunction with the comments of one perhaps more familiar with the question than is Professor Monteil: "Beria was a novice compared with Kazzar, who when questioned boasted that he had tortured to death, or secretly killed, more than two thousand persons. We know now that he was responsible for the killing of innocent

---

[6] Monteil bestows a capital letter on "Gypsies" but not on "jews" and I have respected his usage.
[7] The last words in the quotation are an echo of a celebrated statement made by General de Gaulle at a time, just after the Six-Day War of 1967, when France found it convenient to change sides rather suddenly. The quotation itself is taken from *Le Monde*, Paris, 23–24 March 1969.
[8] *Le Monde*, Paris, 23–24 March 1969.

Jews." The author of this indictment was Mr. El Bakr, sometime President of the Republic of Iraq.[9]

It is in the light of the above that we must judge the strength of Professor Monteil's convictions when he writes: "I am, I repeat, a stranger to anti-Semitism, and detest all forms of racial intolerance. I am speaking here only of the State of Israel, which should be open to criticism like any other State." Who would question this? Professor Monteil himself, when he writes that he cannot "accept the existence of the State of Israel, presented as an accomplished fact."[10]

Ritual Murder—Modern Version

The following example is taken from a communist weekly, *Vie Nuove*,[11] the editors of which we may presume to be scientific materialists and hence unlikely to bring a charge of "ritual murder" against the Jews. It would be well to remember, however, that there is a persistent streak of anti-Semitism in Stalinist and neo-Stalinist ideology. To whom, for instance, do we owe the expression "international Jewish plutocracy"? To Jacques Doriot, no doubt, a French Stalinist before he became a Nazi and a collaborator. But also to Pierre George, a communist academic, in a review which sets out to be "thoughtfully" Marxist.[12] We should remember that pictures representing "The Profanation of the Host" by some exceedingly ugly Jew still decorate the walls of certain Italian churches, despite the efforts made by Italian Jews and a few brave priests to have them removed. However, to return to *Vie Nuove*:

Title of a report from Israel: "Impossible to be a Socialist Citizen of Tel Aviv." In fact, the title is misleading, since the report deals with the efforts Israel is alleged to make to recruit foreign volunteers for its armed forces. This is, as it happens, pure fiction, but even if it were true, the article would be tendentious. Even if the Israeli defence forces had recruited abroad, would that be a crime? There is, after all, such a thing as the French Foreign Legion. This is an excellent example of anti-Zionist "double-speak"—any report, whether true, doubtful, or clearly false, will provide ammunition against Israel. On the other hand, the same acts are perfectly legitimate when attributed to others. Hence, while it is quite all right for the *fedayeen* to enlist fanatical Japanese killers, any appeal by Israel for external assistance is bad by definition. In the same way, an assassin is no longer one if his

[9]*Ibid.*, 11 January 1974.
[10]*Ibid.*, 12 March 1970.
[11]*Vie Nuove* ("Fresh Roads"), organ of the Italian Communist Youth Movement, December 1969.
[12]*La Pensée* ("Thought"), Paris, 1952, p. 140.

victims are "Zionists"—he becomes a "guerrilla" or "freedom fighter"—but because Israel is bad by definition, the motives of those who love, serve, and defend that country can only be evil.

Hence, on seeing a report headed "Impossible to be a Socialist Citizen of Tel Aviv," we must be careful not to fall into the trap. There is no point in taking time and trouble to prove that a *kibbutz* is closer to socialist ideals than a Soviet *kolkhoz* (although the demonstration would not be difficult). Israel does not have to defend itself against the charge of not being socialist enough for the Italian Communist Party. Nor does it have to pander to the King of Saudi Arabia by proving its conservatism.

Here are a few questions for the Italian Communist Party: Is it possible to be a citizen of Mecca and a socialist? Can a Crimean Tartar be a socialist? Would it make sense to inquire whether a citizen of Rome can be a socialist?

There is a serious countercharge to be brought against these young Italians, namely, that persons claiming to be "socialists" have revived the idea of the "ritual murder" which their strongly Catholic ancestors brought against the Jews. For what does the Marxist hold sacred? What corresponds, *mutatis mutandis*, to the Host or the Holy Trinity among Catholics? Surely the Socialist Ideal. Who is the supreme enemy if not the forces ranged against socialism? Those who cannot be socialists become Evil Incarnate. This is especially interesting since from the Marxist point of view it is nonsense to affirm that somebody cannot be a socialist, and thus be deprived of all hope of participation in the Ideal Society, whereas Christianity excludes only the Devil himself from hope, grace, and divine mercy. My next question follows from the above and answers itself: Who, among the nations of the earth, represents Evil Incarnate?

The anti-Zionist press is constantly accusing Israel of crimes of this kind. After Jewish refugees from Morocco had been murdered at Beit Shean, an angry crowd killed their murderers and burnt the corpses. Giorgio Signorini, a pro-communist journalist, describes this as "conspiratorial frenzy and a sacrificial vendetta."[13] Observe the charges brought in these few words; responsibility for conspiracy is shifted to the victims, and responsibility for the "vendetta" as well (although a vendetta traditionally involves two parties). The one party thus accused is also charged with frenzied acts of sacrifice—i.e., of acts both ritual and criminal, if words mean anything.

[13]*Paese Sera*, Rome, 20 November 1974.

Belief in the power of demons always goes hand-in-hand with belief in exorcism. Abdel Malik[14] and others assure us of their desperate efforts to save the Jews from themselves. For such fatherly solicitude, we should be duly grateful.

Original Sin

Readers may ask: "Are the Jews, become Israelis thanks to a change in their fortunes of which you approve, alone blameless? What about Deir Yassin and Kfar Kassem?"

What about them indeed? Deir Yassin is a village whose Arab population was massacred during the Jewish War of Independence in 1948. Kfar Kassem is an Arab village, part of the population of which was killed by an Israeli patrol on the eve of the 1956 war. I shall not go into the facts of the cases, already abundantly exploited by anti-Israeli propaganda and for purposes far removed from the search for truth. The names of these two villages are constantly being brought up by our adversaries, both in and out of context. For the sake of argument, I am prepared to assume the worst of the Israelis, although Arab armies have been similarly guilty from the 1948 war up to the most recent campaign waged by the Kurds against pan-Islamic imperialism, and in the Lebanon the Syrian army was ferocious in breaking the resistance first of the Palestinians, then of the Christians. It is not merely to score a point that I recall the massacre of the entire population of Melouza on 28 May 1957 during the Franco-Algerian war (a massacre committed by the National Liberation Movement, which suspected the village of harbouring rivals) or the vastly more extensive massacres committed by French troops during that war. My one desire is that, ignoring polemics, both sides should come together in an attempt to get to the bottom of the problem.

The accusations made with regard to these two villages, constantly revived by the enemies of Israel, resemble the charge of original sin as brought against the Jews: the sin of being Jewish for the anti-Semite, the sin of being a liberated Jew for the anti-Zionist. The pace of history is constantly accelerating, and it is increasingly true that the more recent the event, the sooner it is erased from the record. Hardly anybody now remembers the execution, without trial, of Imre Nagy by the Russians in 1956 or the massacre of the Ibos in Biafra (1969). Nobody points

[14]Notably in *Le Monde*, Paris, 13 February 1969.

an accusing finger at Algeria because of Melouza. Nobody reminds the French that they once bombed Sétif on a market day. The disputes between France and Algeria today have nothing in common with the furious passions aroused by the Algerian war of independence which ended in 1962. But every effort is made to ensure that Deir Yassin and Kfar Kassem remain a blot on Israel's escutcheon, like the blood on the hands of Lady Macbeth.

The upheavals in contemporary non-Jewish history are marked by incessant shifts of the pendulum. With time, international rancour disappears, new injuries no longer open old wounds, and the tensions which mark international relations are no longer cumulative. In 1945, the Japanese seemed to many Americans little better than devils; today, Japan is thought of as an excellent friend and ally. The change of feeling towards China, too, has been extraordinarily rapid. Only the acts of Israel are laboriously totted up. The history of the Jews, unless it can be subsumed under that of some other people, is presented as a series of unforgotten, unforgiven crimes. No amount of protest by anti-Zionists can withstand the evidence; if after more than a quarter of a century they still brood over Deir Yassin, it is because they share the prejudices of those who, after two thousand years, still hold the Jews guilty of having crucified their Saviour.

The Wandering Jew

Every crime calls for expiation. The unparalleled crime of deicide, according to medieval legend, merited a condemnation to eternal wandering. The legend has been revived by modern anti-Semites in a new form. The Jew must be deprived of all folk-memories and all roots. He must be geographically, as well as physically, vulnerable. As we have seen, this does not prevent history from having been indelibly marked by Jewish misdeeds, while those of other peoples, more fortunate in possessing unchallenged roots in space and time, are allowed to fade.

The innumerable crimes committed against Jews over the centuries, in all sorts of places, are on the contrary readily forgotten. The reasons for the attacks launched on Jewish folk-memories are clear enough; persistent folk-memories enable a people long submerged to start afresh as an organized community and begin once more to play a part in history. This kind of memory is poles apart from the barren commemorative gesture, the old soldiers' procession, the laying of wreaths. The enemies of Israel are on sure ground here. They may tolerate the commemoration of acts which marked the death of Jews, but they permit nothing which might kindle hope in the hearts of the living. At Babi Yar, an immense Jewish charnel house, there is nothing to recall the past (even a poem has been disavowed)[15] for fear that from the vast sufferings endured Jews might derive hope and comfort, and aspire to a share in that glory which the Russians would prefer to keep for themselves; for fear, also, that such memories might foster a sense of kinship among Soviet Jews.

In public debates and television interviews, Israeli diplomats and representatives are often asked by pro-Palestinians what they would do if they were the "humiliated" peoples of Gaza or the West Bank. Apart from the question-begging involved (failure to destroy Israel is "humiliating" to the other camp) and although it never occurs to anyone that a Dalmatian of Italian origin may feel "humiliated" by having to live under a Yugoslav government, the question is either a ruse designed to embarrass or the product of deep-seated unconscious prejudice. Are Nigerians ever invited to put themselves in the place of "humiliated" Biafrans, or Russians told to imagine what it would feel like to be a Czech (or Afghan)?

Similarly, the way in which the media play up the Palestinian refugee problem, when since 1945 the world has seen millions of refugees, puts Israel in the dock but does nothing to help the Palestinians. Those behind such campaigns would be the first to deny that they are in any way influenced by unconscious images of the Wandering Jew. Nevertheless, they cannot bear the thought that the sentence passed on him should have been quashed, and above all they cannot bear to think of the Jews as having displaced any other people.

Pending the physical destruction of Israel, still unattainable although eagerly desired, the process of eliminating Israel and its inhabitants from our mental world continues. An "Appeal on Behalf of the Palestinians" published in the French press breaks with custom in not putting the word "Israeli" in quotation marks (a device much favoured by French newspapers in speaking of something the legitimacy of which they question; thus, during the Franco-Algerian war, the "Provisional Government of the Algerian Republic" was never mentioned without the quotation marks). When, nevertheless, it has to refer to the Israelis, the appeal talks about the "present inhabitants of Palestine." There could be no more

---

[15] In "Babi Yar" (*Literaturnaya Gazeta*, Moscow, 10 September 1961) the Soviet poet Y. Yevtushenko denounced official anti-Semites for their refusal to recognize the martyrdom of Jews. His attitude was violently denounced by Nikita Khrushchev (*Pravda*, Moscow, 8 March 1963).

eloquent expression of the boundless contempt in which the anti-Semite holds the Jews, condemned to wander but condemned for wandering. The Jews happen to be somewhere by chance, but only provisionally, since they have no right to be anywhere, except by-your-leave. Or they are where they are for the basest of motives—"inhabitants" if you will, but provisional only, the hope being that something will be done to drive them out or otherwise eliminate their presence, or to bring about their absorption in a "democratic" State in which they would once again be a despised minority.

In the anti-Zionist mind, therefore, the idea of culpability which has played so strong a part in shaping anti-Jewish imagery throughout the ages has been shifted not merely to Israel as a Jewish country but to its "present inhabitants." Yet this shift has not appeared overnight. In the last hundred years or so, with the decline in religious belief, the various traditional accretions to the Christian faith, including the idea of a people condemned to eternal punishment for the crime of deicide, have gradually faded from men's minds; among the more sophisticated, the process has been assisted by developments in Biblical scholarship. The very real massacre of Jews during the Second World War was vaguely felt to be an adequate expiation of any possible guilt. Thus it was that the emergence of the State of Israel was accompanied by a wave of sympathy which seemed to indicate that the legend had at long last worn itself out: the Wandering Jew had reached a safe haven.

A generation has passed, the crematoria chimneys smoke no longer, and many hearts are no longer sensitive. The Jew, who thought he had at last escaped the Curse, is once more in the dock. Until recently, the traditional charge he had to face was one of rootless cosmopolitanism; today, his attempts to reestablish roots, even in Jerusalem (a city as sacred to Jews as Mecca is to Moslems), are held against him.

Only the traditional imagery has changed; overt anti-Jewish sentiments have gone out of fashion. Anti-Semitism has found a new and more respectable ideal—the cause of revolution.

Anti-Zionism of Christian Origin

Revolution has served as a slogan to cover a multitude of sins—especially in Russia since 1917. It has taken a long time, the genius of a Solzhenitsin, and a new political philosophy to sow the seeds of doubt in Western left-wing opinion and for the countless crimes and blunders committed in the name of Revolution to be recognized. It is clear by now that revolutionary ideology is unable to provide a solution for the Jewish problem; hence I devote no special chapter to Marxist anti-Zionism. There are anti-Zionist Marxists, but they draw their inspirations from elsewhere.

Christian anti-Zionism is quite a different matter. There is a long tradition of Christian anti-Jewish feeling, an abundant literature, much popular imagery, and above all the fact that Christianity began when it broke away from its Jewish roots. An honourable past proves nothing in this connection. Certain anti-Zionists make play out of the assistance given to Jews under the Third Reich (whether prompted by Christian charity or given for political motives, as a manifestation of solidarity in the face of Nazism). For psychological rather than political motives, these anti-Zionists stopped feeling sympathy for the Jews once persecution ceased. The anti-Zionist finds it intolerable that the Jews should no longer be reduced to soliciting aid and protection. Georges Montaron, editor of the French journal *Témoignage chrétien* ("Christian Witness"), claims to have protected Jewish unfortunates at a time when such help was needed, and on this I am happy to congratulate him, if congratulations are in order. I do, however, earnestly hope that never again will he have occasion to display such magnanimity. Circumstances such as those in which his aid was given may provide an occasion for the exercise of the Christian virtues; for the Jew, they smell of death.

The Christian anti-Zionists sometimes argue that the West too easily rid itself of guilt by accepting the State of Israel in 1948. What was sometimes murmured at that time became a proclaimed conviction after 1967. The Jews, it would seem, have forfeited that sympathy which the West, moved by Christian charity and in expiation of past wrongs, would willingly extend, and today can regain it only by opposition to the existence of Israel. Until they are prepared to do so, these same Christians will support the Arab world and will be prepared, at the most, to offer the Jews a provisional, revocable right to personal security. But those who give aid and succor to the *fedayeen* in the belief that the lot of the Palestinians in Israel is comparable to that of the Jews under Hitler should spend a couple of months in Israeli-administered Judaea and then a few days in the concentration camps of certain "progressive" countries (and I trust none of them compares in horror to Auschwitz) to acquire some standards for comparison. If their initial support for Israel was justified, they are being inconsistent, as they are inconsistent when they now assert that the Jews can aspire to no more than assimilation in an Arab mass, or when they call for the transfer of all authority to the Palestinian Arabs, to the detriment, even, of those Jews who had been in Palestine before the Arabs arrived (the Jews of Safed, for instance, whose children were killed at Maalot on 15 May 1974), or of the Jewish refugees, especially those from the Arab countries (such as those massacred at Kiryat Shemona on 11 April 1974).

Where does Christ come into all this? We are getting there. The Christian anti-Zionist press began by insinuating, and has since proclaimed, that "Christ was a Palestinian." Ethnologically, historically, these words of course mean nothing. But consider the implications! The Inquisition at the height of its power showed no greater mastery of innuendo in instilling into Christian minds the idea of Jewish guilt for the death of God.

It is difficult, of course, to be quite as blunt as this. "Certain persons," we read (some of them were French ecclesiastics),

> wish to denounce those who by repeatedly alleging that there has been a rebirth of anti-Semitism in France, seek to transfer the odium to the opponents of the racialist and expansionist policies of a State, namely, the State of Israel. Such allegations serve the purpose of Zionist propaganda in that they foster a sense of alarm and despondency among Frenchmen of Jewish faith or origins and hence stimulate migration to Israel.[16]

Here we have, it seems, Christians who can with a straight face assert that anti-Semitism is an invention of Zionist propaganda.

Father Robert Davezies, a French Roman Catholic priest, who with me had opposed the Algerian war, signed this declaration along with a number of anti-Semites of the extreme Right. He thus takes us back, through fashionable "progressive" Christianity, to the older, now officially discarded anti-Judaism of the Roman Catholic Church.

At a time when he did not consider me to be tainted by racism, I had asked Father Davezies to approach his "Black Power" American friends and try to make their leader Stokely Carmichael understand what the struggle for Jewish liberation meant, instead of mouthing slogans which came near to outright anti-Semitism. Father Davezies promised to think about it. He must be thinking about it still. In

---

[16]*Le Monde*, Paris, 13 December 1969.

52   THE ANTI-ZIONIST COMPLEX

the meantime Carmichael has gone on record as saying: "I have never admired a White man, but the greatest of them, to my mind, was Hitler."[17]

The editors of *Témoignage chrétien* add a gloss to the piece of wisdom mentioned above. Father Biot, for instance, maintains that Zionists condemn themselves by "placing themselves outside the faith in the Risen Christ."[18] What about the Moslems, then? L. Séguillon seems to imply the theological superiority of Islam in an article headed "Islam and Jerusalem"in the same issue:

> The true cult thus to some extent became the property of the Jews, who claimed to be the only heirs to the Promise of Abraham. Once their sense of property has prevailed in this way, God—Infinite though He be—is reduced to the status of an object.

This is an extraordinary assertion. Has the Catholic Church (for instance) never claimed exclusive possession of religious truth? As to Islam, when Hebron was under Arab sovereignty, no Jew was granted access to the Tomb of Abraham, and even today it is doubtful whether an Unbeliever discovered in Mecca would escape with his life, whereas the Israeli city of Jerusalem is freely open to people of all religions.

The following statement by G. Montaron, again, is remarkably revealing: "The State of Israel seeks aggrandizement by force of arms, ejecting the Palestinians to establish a specifically Jewish entity in the name of the Bible." A Jewish victory becomes a Manichaean vision of Evil expelling Good. What is most revealing here is the condemnation out-of-hand of a specifically Jewish State. The fact that there are twenty-odd specifically Moslem States, and many others of Christian inspiration (the Church of England is subsidized by the State, its bishops are nominated by the Prime Minister, and it is the church to which the reigning monarch always belongs), is passed over as irrelevant. An aggravating circumstance, for these Christian witnesses, is that the Israelis are impudent enough to derive their inspiration from the Bible and to claim spiritual descent in direct line from the people whose doings are chronicled therein. This is enough to justify a charge of "racist theocracy."

The Christian anti-Zionists are fond of condemning Israel for its "confusion of

---

[17]*New York Times*, 14 April 1970.
[18]*Témoignage chrétien*, 7 May 1970.

the temporal and the sacred." In fact, the history of every people is a mixture of the two. The very idea of nationhood, with its national flags, national anthems, and other patriotic symbols, embodies such a mixture; countries—other than Israel—are usually complimented on having achieved a successful blend. Even Marxist internationalism, such as it is (and such as it is imposed), with its myths, its liturgy, its dogmas and its casuistry, is a permanent "confusion" of temporal and sacred. Is it not rather because the Jews are the original people of the Bible that they are, by Christians of this kind (and by Moslems), denied the right to their sacred symbols and their sacred book?

A Self-Negating Anti-Zionism

While moderate anti-Zionists can invoke the universal character of Judaism, Jews who join forces with the PLO in abominating everything to do with Israel— PLO fellow-travellers—have nothing similar to fall back on. They illustrate a form of self-negation and self-abasement frequently encountered among long-persecuted minorities. Whence an incoherence, sometimes carried to the point of delirium, in their thought and its expression. When an admirer of the *fedayeen* who happens to be a rabbi (such a one exists!) invokes cabalistic calculation to explain the six million Jewish dead "by the fact that Man was created on the Sixth Day," it is clear to all that the man is mad. But when, in *Le Nouvel Observateur*,[19] P. Vidal-Naquet, who is not mad, gravely reviews the piece of ineptitude from which these words are quoted, it becomes painfully obvious how far the critical sense of even the most moderate anti-Zionist can become blunted. That Jewish communities should have their morbid fringe is not in itself surprising; indeed, the phenomenon might even be taken as evidence for the continued vitality of the Jewish people. Far from remaining inert amid global upheavals, Jews act as agents of history. But there is a wastage: a reviving nation, conscious of its powers, is a living body from which the dead scales drop, like dead leaves from a tree shaken by the wind.

The behaviour of anti-Zionist Jews clearly reveals a rejection of themselves as Jews and an unconscious acquiescence in the image which their enemies seek to project of them. The process is psychologically understandable, but is a

[19]*Le Nouvel Observateur*, 10 November 1969.

form of political defeatism. For if all oppressed peoples reacted in the same perverse way, seeking to identify themselves with a supposedly inflexible oppressor, national emancipation would be an impossibility.

For such Jewish anti-Zionists, those Jews who are interested in the national liberation of the Jewish people are pursuing a will-o'-the-wisp. The anti-Zionists fail to understand that national liberation implies legitimate self-defence and the defence of Judaism. The vicissitudes of the Diaspora have brought about a state of affairs in which many marginal Jews are interested in neither the one nor the other. Some lose their sense of identity and any residual loyalty they might owe to other Jews and proclaim a shocking solidarity with those who bring death to their brethren. One French Jew urges us to "kneel and kiss the feet of the *fedayeen*"; another rejoices "that machine-guns splutter and grenades explode on Palestinian soil." I shall be charitable enough not to name them; it is not my job to replace national authorities in a task they seem reluctant to undertake, namely, penalizing incitement to mass murder. I merely take leave to reflect on the fate of Abraham Serfaty, a Moroccan Jew and a violent anti-Zionist, director of the review *Souffles* published in Rabat. Arrested and tortured by the Moroccan police, he has given the following account of what he had to endure: "One inspector, whose appearance I carefully noted, said to me in Arabic, having copiously insulted Jews in general: 'We got rid of Mehdi Ben Barka;[20] after him, you'll be no problem.' " A Mr. Bloch, professing to be "an anti-Zionist Jew," in a letter published in *Le Monde*, protests at length against Serfaty's detention but vehemently condemns not, as might have been expected, the Moroccan authorities but "the poison of Zionism."

All this is less surprising than distressing. But to invite us to follow the lead of Jews such as these, who admit to being Jews only so that they may the more effectively oppose any expression of a national will, is like holding up strike-breakers as models for the working class. In all minority communities, certain individuals come to see themselves through the eyes of the majority and make desperate efforts to avoid identification with a disagreeable image. The mirror in which they try so hard to admire themselves is sometimes reproachful, sometimes comforting, subject to the rules of the shadow game they play. They are in very truth pursuing a will-o'-the-wisp.

---

[20] A noted leader of the Moroccan opposition, abducted in Paris by the King's agents and never seen again.

The history of the Jews is unfortunately only too full of cases such as these, in which individual Jews display a lack of backbone, as shown by the following quotation from the late Gilbert Mury: "Those who persistently equate 'Jew' with 'Israeli' are Zionist fanatics, in odious agreement with the Nazis in holding that French Jews are Jews and not French citizens."[21]

It is of course obvious that the German occupation authorities in France, in insisting on this distinction, were—contrary to the Zionists—not in the least concerned (very much the reverse) with the salvation of the Jews, and that the author of the quotation is either speaking from ignorance or arguing in bad faith, i.e., trying to transfer to Zionists the opprobrium attached to Nazism, while hoping that the reader will not notice the sleight of hand. On the whole, historical ignorance and over-simplification are as much a characteristic of the extreme anti-Zionist as psychological tortuousness is of the moderate.

The pro-Palestinian Jew sometimes professes a lyrical admiration for the *fedayeen*. "Except for their lives, Palestinians have nothing to lose. Nothing, you understand?"[22] What I understand from this piece of rhetoric is the extraordinary political immaturity of the writer. There is a striking precedent: in 1938 we were told that the Sudeten German minority in Czechoslovakia had nothing to lose, Hitler having decided that the existing state of affairs was intolerable. We all know what the consequences were. Unlike the Jews, the Palestinians have never in fact been in a position in which "they had nothing to lose"; and to say that they are in such a position now is to push them into an adventure with potentially disastrous consequences. Authors such as these, if really concerned with helping the Palestinians and not just working off their own complexes, would begin by putting the problem in political terms. They might, for instance, try to persuade the Palestinians that Israel exists, and exists legitimately, and hence that to come to terms with this reality would involve no shame, but would rather redound to their own advantage. Such realism is even more necessary after the massacres of Palestinians by Jordanians and Syrians, and especially now that Israel and Egypt have begun to move along the road to a peaceful settlement despite all advice from "good friends" who seek to nip in the bud the chance—perhaps the last chance—of peace.

[21]*Le Monde*, Paris, 18 September 1972.
[22]Jérôme Lindon, in the preface to *Pour les Fidayine*, by Jacques Vergès, Editions de Minuit, Paris.

Despite the view that Egypt may be sliding towards a role inconsistent with its history—that of "brandishing the sword of imperialism in alliance with Israel, with a view to strangling Arab nationalism"[23]—President Sadat's initiative and subsequent developments show that the road to peace, although not easy, is practicable. This is no time to set up fresh hurdles which would make things harder for one or the other party. The position between the Mediterranean and the Jordan could be at least no more tense than is the case in other areas inhabited by two or more peoples; indeed, less so. Such areas are not uncommon in Europe itself (witness the Istrian Peninsula, Transylvania, Macedonia). The Palestinians, perhaps even more than the Israelis, have everything to gain and nothing to lose in seeking to advance beyond the sterile antagonism which the enemies of Israel and the enemies of peace (they are the same) seek to perpetuate. The words "have nothing to lose" could more appropriately be applied to the Syrian Jews, who live in the hope of repatriation to Eretz Israel.

I ought, it may be said, to have based the above judgments on political rather than on psychological grounds. I might have classified anti-Zionist Jews according to their political options, which range from a touchy loyalty to their local non-Jewish community to an internationally inclined ultra-Leftism. The advantage of the psychological analysis is that it offers criteria more solid than those which rely on the political choices made by the Jews of the Diaspora. History is there to show that the loyalty displayed by Jews to a particular nation or international movement tends to be one-sided and precarious, with no guarantee whatever that the nation or movement so favoured will reciprocate by showing consideration for Jewish interests.

The insistence shown by so many Jews in wishing themselves other than they are, in refusing to see the reasons for their common misfortune, and in being blind to the difficult splendour of a Jewish vocation, is an indication of a deep-seated spiritual malaise. These Jews will remain prisoners of the resulting contradictions as long as they refuse to accept themselves for what they are. Self-awareness and political commitment must go hand-in-hand.

I am more interested in this awareness and in the possibility of a political solution than in the psychology of these purblind Jews, whom I have little hope of converting. How these people square matters with their own conscience is a matter of indifference to me; I oppose them only to the extent that they deny the existence

---

[23]Mme M. C. Aulas, *Le Monde diplomatique,* December 1977.

of a Jewish identity and disallow the creation of a Jewish State. If "Zionist propaganda" were all it is made out to be, no anti-Zionist statement by such people would remain unchallenged. It is sometimes held to the credit of Judaism that it tolerates every school of thought, even rabid anti-Zionism. It is certainly to the credit of Zionism that — unlike the PLO — it does not seek to silence its critics by threats or worse.

It is nothing less than pathetic that Jews who have transferred their allegiance to the other camp believe that in attacking Israel and seeking to encompass its destruction they are, in their own fashion, combatting anti-Semitism — as if it were possible to advance the cause of freedom by choosing to remain unfree. Persecuted themselves, the would-be persecutors of others, they find their enemies, not in their self-styled well-wishers, but in those they are willing to betray.

It is pathetic that Israel, relentlessly criticized by these people, should in the long run be their only shield and refuge and, paradoxically, the only real guarantee of their right to speak out, even though what they say runs counter to their own interests.

Finally, it is pathetic (but Jewish history is full of such pathos) that these persons, whether they like it or not, and whether I like it or not (and God knows how earnestly, at times, I wish it were not so), remain my brethren.

The Myth of Assimilation and Non-Mythical Assimilation

The myth of assimilation still commands belief, though constantly and clearly proved fallacious by history. I say "myth"; rather is it a mirage, a comforting way out of present difficulties, a straw at which a drowning man may clutch. It has nothing glorious about it, nor is it genuinely desired by the assimilators (although the columns of the anti-Zionist press will be thrown wide open to the renegade). The candidates for assimilation win something different — the right to go down in some leaky old tub between two equally hostile ports, to disappear in no-man's land between two frontiers, or in a gas chamber; or, with a little luck, to rot in the holds of such old ships as stay afloat or in some internment camp. In the best of cases, it means acceptance by, and subordination to, foreign non-Jewish interests, the Jew being accepted only so long as he refrains from expressing the slightest solidarity with other Jews. The point is reinforced by polemics about the alleged "double allegiance" of the Jews: in England, the doubts entertained in 1914 as to whether Jews, most of whom bore German-sounding names, could really be depended on to share the enthusiastic belligerency of their country of adoption; in France, on the occasion of the Six-Day War of 1967, with the government's sudden shift of policy to a pro-Arab line.

In so far as the individual deliberately chooses assimilation, I am bound to respect his choice. But I oppose assimilation as a policy because, contrary to what its champions believe or would have us believe, it in no way brings nearer the advent of a world-wide republic; rather does it reinforce the ethnocentrism of other peoples to the detriment of the Jews alone. Throughout the ages, and especially since the events of this century, many Jews have dreamt of escaping from the cycle of persecution-toleration. This dream the assimilationist fails to see, or seeing, denies, and remains unmoved by a natural human reaction to an intolerable threat. He is moved neither by the humiliation of the Jews nor by the spiritual force of Judaism. He is prepared to recognize only non-Jewish culture and traditions as authentic and considers Judaism as their marginal subproduct. But let the Jewish people—held to be nonexistent—assert its will to exist, and it is immediately held responsible and accused of guilt towards these other peoples. Such contradictions are characteristic of a way of thought which refuses to recognize realities and obstinately persists in according the status of reality to fiction.

If there is such a thing as authentic assimilation, a living, developing reality, it is that whereby the Jews of Palestine have attached themselves to their soil and shouldered their vocation as a nation, rejecting dispersion and assimilation as the only possible alternative. Just as the classical anti-Semite would willingly abolish everything Jewish as detrimental to non-Jews, so the extreme anti-Zionist regards all evidence of a Jewish national existence as "aggression" or a trespass on the rights of others. The French Arabist Jacques Berque settles the question once and for all: "Israeli excesses have made Israeli usurpation unpardonable."[24]

For the Jews, the choice is to be landless and rootless or to possess some 8,000 square miles of land which two thousand years ago had been part of their own; moreover, it is land they have purchased. For the Arabs, the choice is between more than 4 million square miles minus these 8,000, and the 4 million intact, reputedly inalienably Arab by right, even if the intact 4 million should leave another people perpetually rootless. Any Jewish presence whatever, for those who

[24] J. Berque et al., *Les Palestiniens et la crise israélo-arabe*, Editions sociales, Paris, 1974, p. 31.

favour this latter option, is a trespass, even if the Jews are to be found only on land the reclamation of which is entirely the work of Jewish hands: the Negev Desert, rescued from the oblivion and neglect which had been its fate ever since the sands closed over the Hebrew vestiges beneath; the ruins of Massada, a monument to the Jewish struggle against the Roman invader, allowed to rot (with the entire surrounding area) for centuries; the town of Arad, driving its roots down to the underground water supplies mentioned in Biblical accounts and Hebrew inscriptions; the cities of Jerusalem, Safed and Tiberias, where the majority of the population, despite massacre and expulsion, has always been Jewish. I quote from an anti-Zionist pamphlet.

> 1912: in Tiberias, 7,500 people lived in harmony, three-quarters of them Jews (with seven synagogues), 1,600 Moslems and 260 Christians .... Safed, a town of 20,000 souls, the majority of them Jews .... Jerusalem, the 70,000 inhabitants of which officially comprised 10,000 Moslems, 15,000 Christians and 45,000 Jews.[25]

This state of affairs is clearly not to the liking of another specialist in political fiction, the "Political Director" of a journal calling itself *Revue d'étude des relations internationales* ("Journal for the Study of International Relations"), published in Paris, who asserts that: "Since 1947, the history of Jerusalem has been that of an Arab city of which its legitimate sovereign has been despoiled." There is something familiar about the axe this specialist has to grind, for a few lines further on we read: "In fact, Jerusalem, a Holy City, is also, and above all, an Arab town. A Holy Place in which the Spirit walks, it does not exist remote from the contingencies of time and space. It is a city of men and women."[26]

Doubtless the Jewish inhabitants of Jerusalem, even if they happen to constitute a majority, do not qualify as "men and women." Of course a "Holy City" (in which, moreover, "the Spirit walks") cannot have been, cannot now be, and cannot remain Jewish. And this of a city whose sanctity goes back at least to David and the building of the Temple by Solomon. However, we cannot be sure how

---

[25] G. Vaucher, *Document Palestine*, No. 2, Geneva. This is designed to prove that Jews and Moslems lived together in peace and harmony, and would have continued so to live, had it not been for the unfortunate creation of Israel.
[26] Ch. Saint-Prot, *Jérusalem, ville arabe* ("Jerusalem, an Arab City"), in *Le Monde*, Paris, 14 August 1980.

much weight this objection would carry with the learned author, who would doubtless claim both these Kings of Israel as ancestors of Yasser Arafat and King Hussein.

Other peoples are granted a natural and inalienable right to a national identity simply because they are where they are. In most cases they are there, ultimately, by right of conquest. There have been a very few instances in which the local people have been consulted about their fate (as in Savoy and the Saar), but land settlement throughout history is one long story of forceful evictions, occupation by the successful invaders being in the course of time accepted and granted international recognition.

Historical upheavals create victims and vanquished, majorities and minorities, and balances which may or may not prove lasting. The stronger party, with a clear conscience, demands submission from the weaker, putting down (as the Turks have done with the Armenians) any attempt to review what it considers the verdict of history. Nobody, and certainly not the anti-Zionist, expects any other kind of behaviour. Nobody expects the President of Algeria or the President of Iraq, for instance, to recognize the preemptive rights of Algerian Berber Jews, or those of the survivors of the exodus from Babylon, to land which belonged to their ancestors well before their Arab Moslem compatriots arrived on the scene.

By forfeiting their rights in Israel, the Jews would be left with no historical rights anywhere and would remain perpetually dependent on the goodwill of others. Provided these latter were prepared to accept a Jewish presence in *mellah* or *ghetto*, not even a protest would be in order; the Jews would simply have to adapt themselves to an alien context.

No form of specifically Jewish defence is allowed in reaction to anti-Jewish persecution, humiliation, or threats. A defence is acceptable only if made in the name of the vaguest of humanitarian principles, or if accompanied by a profession of faith in socialism, or by tributes to the Founding Fathers and the Constitution, or if preceded by conversion to something radically different (Islam, Christianity, a Palestinian "secular State," or what you will). To defend himself against persecution for what he had been and no longer is, the Jew who takes this course will have to rely entirely on the entity or cause to which he has thus transferred his allegiance.

For the anti-Zionist, it is merely a regrettable fact of history (but one from which no lessons, and in particular no conclusions as to the need for a national home, may on any account be drawn) that the survivors of the greatest massacre in modern history should be crowded together on the deck of the *Exodus* in quest of a homeland, then returned to former German concentration camps after having been fired on by British troops; and that some of them should afterwards have been victims of fresh pogroms in socialist Poland.

The distinction between "nation" and "State"—which the anti-Zionist likes to make against Israel (one of the oldest nations in the world)—is never used in criticism of any of the scores of newly created States whose national unity is far from evident. Where a true nation exists but is forcibly embodied in some other (often artificial) national entity, we behold revolts bloodily put down (Biafra) or suppression by mass deportation or forced assimilation (in Iraq, Iran and Turkey; all these measures, or combinations thereof, have been applied against the long-suffering Kurds). But suppression and ethnocide, when practised by Nigerians, Iraqis, Iranians or Turks, are promptly shrugged off by the same people who will seize on any pretext to embarrass Israel or devote whole columns in the press to the expulsion by that country of a single Palestinian. Nigeria, Iraq, Turkey and Iran are recognized as existing by right, but it is considered almost indecent to claim legitimacy for the Jewish State.

Those who are being generously armed to challenge this claim, whether the weapons be supplied in the name of Christ, Mohammed or Marx, and whether such persons be called terrorists or freedom fighters, their efforts are doomed to failure. Not because, as the more rabid anti-Zionists would have us believe, they are confronted with a particularly ferocious and unscrupulous opponent, but because they are confronted with a resistance more determined, more legitimate than their own. Because no people has had to suffer so much and so long as the people of Israel. Because Israeli stubbornness is hardened by denial of Israel's legitimacy and by threats to Israel's existence. Israelis, the vanguard of the Jewish people, aspire to remain alive, not to take life. They stand to lose everything, and they know it.

The "Destruction of Zionist Structures"

The reason for the victories of Israel and for Israel's persistence in remaining true to itself (a triumph greater by far than any military success) is not to be sought in Israeli courage alone. It is a mystery only to those who associate Israel with all sorts of sinister occult forces and carry around in their heads that image of the Jews which the authors of the *Protocols of the Elders of Zion* deliberately tried to project. The mystery, if there is one, lies in those "structures" which it is claimed must be destroyed.[27] For the Israeli, however, they represent the indivisible totality of his country, his life under the skies of Israel, his roots in the soil, memories regained and memories erased—a continuous process in which contingencies can be attended to without any loss of the long-term view, and the guarantee of a continuity in which every link represents creation, affirmation, and defiance of death. All these things are covered by what are called "Zionist structures." To damage any one dimension in them is to damage them all.

This means that Israel is vulnerable. The more ambitious the project, the greater the risk of failure and disappointment. But we are not thereby justified in condemning any great enterprise in advance as either rash or unnecessary. To reassert a national identity and to resurrect a State was essential if a decimated and humiliated people was to be spared further, intolerable, trials. But it was inevitable that other trials should threaten, precisely because what was being resurrected was Jewish national power.

That power is real, though often exaggerated or given a sinister connotation. From the beginning, the political, economic and military aspects have frequently been interpreted—deliberately or not—as a threat to others. But the dangers run by a newly reunited nation are less than those incurred by a people scattered, disarmed, and impotent.

I am not naive enough to imagine that I am alone in facing risks in the world today. I observe that other communities are dominated, not only by quantifiable interests, but also, more often, by prejudice, fantasy, sometimes hysteria, making the future impossible to predict. In such a world, I refuse the dubious virtue of objectivity.

Am I exaggerating? Perhaps. Possibly the ups-and-downs in Jewish history have

---

[27]Statement by the Unified Command of the Palestinian Resistance Movement Declaring a Formula for National Unity and a Programme for Political and Military Action (Amman, Jordan, 6 May 1970), paragraph 12: "Israel, by virtue of its structure, is a closed racialist society linked with imperialism, and also, by virtue of its *structure*, the limited progressive forces that exist in it are incapable of bringing about any radical change in the character of Israel as a Zionist racialist State linked with imperialism. Therefore the aim of the Palestinian revolution is to liquidate this entity in all its aspects, political, military, social, trade unions and cultural, and to liberate Palestine completely."

been no more than accidents. As a Jew, part of me maintains an uneasy vigilance, and part is dominated by the urge to forget. This latter part would like nothing so much as to surrender to that confident optimism without which, certainly, life is much grimmer. But I am taking a risk if I yield to the temptation and slacken my vigilance. It is therefore criminal on the part of those who stand on the sidelines to urge me to drop my guard, for the result—for me and other Jews like me—might be death. Those who claim to be objective, and can afford this luxury—let them take their cue from Baghdad or Moscow, and tell me who will step in to prevent the deaths of Jews next time.

Who, if not ourselves, in the only way open to us. Thanks to "structures"—simultaneously living and indestructible.

IV
The Ways of Repression

The unprovoked attacks launched against Israel, whether against the State itself or its subjects, all derive from the same deliberate attempt at repression—repression of any aspiration towards emancipation of the Jewish people, in the Diaspora or in the resurrected homeland; repression which, alternating with periods of paternalism and condescension, has been a constant feature of the policy of many countries towards the Jews. The repression attempted is total when part of this people, refusing both protection and persecution, lays the foundation for national emancipation and proclaims its independence. In the last resort it is repression of the people which proclaims the messianic hope and of the challenge that hope represents.[1]

Just as the key victory of the Second World War, at Stalingrad (1943)—warmly welcomed as it was—did nothing to settle postwar problems and in fact laid the foundations for the cold war, so the victories of Israeli arms have not solved the problems arising from the presence of the Jewish people in the world, and have indeed created new ones. In recent years, an increasing number of people have come to feel an Israeli victory to be an embarrassment (although they would never

---

[1] I shall return to this in Chapter VI.

question the victory at Stalingrad). Those who believe that their interests are not served by Israeli victories, or harbour some unconscious anti-Jewish resentment, are all too ready to go further and declare such victories undesirable.

For such as these, the emancipation of the persecuted Jews of the Soviet Union, their opposition to one of the best-organized of all police States, and their reabsorption into a homeland which resurrects the Israel of old, reveal some sinister unconfessed imperialism. In other words, what is an understandable human phenomenon is perceived as inhuman because Jewish by those who are themselves inhuman (or become so because they are anti-Zionists). There are of course reasons which help to explain this attitude. Very few people know anything at all about Jewish history; information about Middle Eastern affairs in general is inadequate; and the oil blackmail clearly plays an important part as well. But there are deeper reasons.

Are we in turn going to surrender because of unfavourable trends in public opinion? The chairman at one of my lectures, introducing me to the audience, thought it would be well (his intentions were of the best) to avoid any allusion to the fact that my whole family had been exterminated during the Second World War. I interrupted him: "Does this mean that Jews are no longer entitled to mention their misfortunes?" He had tried, *ad usum populi*, to skate over something which has been a constant feature in Jewish history throughout the ages—something we must never forget.

"We"? For long I detested this pronoun, used to justify any fanatical belief by those who would fain submerge their personal inadequacies in some collective pool, endowed with imaginary plenitude. It was some time before I grasped that the "we" which is no mere figure of speech but a fact of life can be a real source of plenitude—that plenitude which life confers on us and hence runs a constant risk of death. The "we" used by the oppressed, the ghetto folk, the so-called inferior races, represents a real brotherhood (not always an honourable one) in which one's neighbour is one's brother for better and certainly for worse. Unfortunately, any confraternity has its own fair share of fools, smart alecks and turncoats. The difference here is that whether they like it or not, all are stamped with the mark of a misfortune which cannot be exchanged, redeemed, or shifted to other shoulders, and remains a permanent feature of the community throughout its history. The burden cannot be got rid of by abandoning the community, nor by disguise, nor by sleight of hand.

Being Black and Being Jewish

However, from time to time in history conversion to the dominant ideology has appeared a promising avenue of escape (although, under the Inquisition, the Catholic Church was for long highly suspicious of converts, who had to display quite special zeal). At about the same time and until quite recently, skin colour became an adequate reason for enslavement or extermination. Hitler extended the idea of race to the converted Jews, who were gassed and incinerated like the others. In a sense, the racial prejudice of socialist Poland marks an advance on that of Hitler's Germany. The persons expelled have included Catholics, who on the station platform have learnt to their amazement that they were descendants of the Frankists, i.e., the disciples of the false Messiah Jacob Frank (1720–1791), who had followed their master's example by embracing Christianity.

Today, if it is fashionable to do so or if he feels the need, a communist can become a Christian, the Christian an atheist, the Hindu a Moslem. The Black and the Jew, however, for those who hate and despise them, remain hateful and despicable forever. Similarly, in accordance with the ups and downs of politics, X will be forgiven for having been this or that, Y for not having been this or that. Both X and Y will congratulate themselves for remaining alive after having stupidly been at each other's throat before the XXth Party Congress.[2] They may well find themselves at daggers drawn again if the party line should change. But there is no prescription for Black or Jew.

Here the paths of Black and Jew diverge. I shall confine myself to the political lessons we can learn from this, overlooking contingencies, however painful they may have been for those concerned. We live in an age when clear dividing-lines have been blurred. But, at least, the process known as "decolonization" has won universal approval. Not that decolonization has had particularly gratifying results in certain newly independent countries, such as Uganda or Nigeria; not that, from South Africa to the run-down suburbs and coloured ghettos of the Western world, the stark realities of second-class status have been seriously challenged. But one point at any rate has been established: nobody today, apart from the frank reactionary, would seriously maintain that oppression of coloured peoples is a historical necessity or can be justified by reference to Divine Decree.

---

[2] At the XXth Congress of the Soviet Communist Party in 1956, Khrushchev, in a celebrated secret report, revealed Stalin's misdeeds.

But the position of the Jews has remained unaffected. In the hope that any conclusions reached will be consistent, let us consider the Western world alone, i.e., that part of the world in which the lot of the Jewish Diaspora is most enviable. Let us overlook the occasional evidence to the contrary and agree that the movement towards Jewish emancipation, begun in the nineteenth century, is now irreversible. Has not Spain, the mother of the Inquisition, opened its frontiers to Jews? (Admittedly, in December 1976, a Libyan warning deterred the King of that proud country from greeting the delegates to the World Jewish Congress, meeting for the first time in Madrid.) Let us agree that the Third Reich was no more than a parenthesis, now closed, and take note with satisfaction that tribute is now paid to the memory of our martyrs, despite the fact that from time to time eccentric historians claim that the gas chambers never existed. Let us assume that the anti-Semitic rumours in Orleans (which by May 1969 had assumed such proportions that the French authorities were obliged to intervene),[3] the desecration of Jewish cemeteries, the scribblings and threats which flourish in France and elsewhere rightly belong to the miscellaneous news columns of the local press. Let us even have the courage to consider as in no way outside the normal run of events the attack which wounded twenty-six young people at a Jewish students' residence in Paris on 27 March 1979. Or the grenades lobbed into a group of Jewish children in Antwerp (26 July 1980) by an Arab who managed to kill one boy and wound twenty others (he pleaded that "his gesture was to be judged in the context of the Arab-Israeli dispute").[4] Or the bomb attack of 3 October 1980, as a result of which four persons died and some fifteen were injured, outside the synagogue in the Rue Copernic in Paris. Let us forget that the deep-rooted prejudices which in the past led to charges of ritual murder or deicide have to some extent been shifted from the Jews as a people to the State of Israel.

It remains true, however—and this is essential—that in so far as the need for a Jewish national home—the State of Israel—is not felt to be imperative, public opinion feels it right and proper that the Jewish people should be refused independence, whereas the existence of other non-independent peoples is felt to be the scandalous reminder of an evil past. Certainly much progress has been made since President Sadat's visit to Israel, with *de facto* then *de jure* recognition, and direct contacts. For the *raïs*, for the Egyptian people, for all supporters of the

---

[3]See Edgar Morin, *Rumour in Orleans*, Blond, London, 1971.
[4]*France-Soir*, Paris, 28 July 1980.

THE WAYS OF REPRESSION   69

new line, and in a sense for the whole international community, a new and different approach has been tried. Nevertheless, even if the existence of Israel is no longer seriously questioned, public opinion still fails to grasp that existence means nothing unless it is secure, with the result that Israel's security claims, such as the maintenance of a few Jewish settlements in the desert, encounter general disapproval. It is not my concern to decide whether in this respect the policies adopted by the government of Israel are wise or not. I would simply make the point that while public opinion is constantly critical, or at the best suspicious, of Israel and is hostile to the Soviet Union when that country undertakes operations of a spectacular kind (Hungary, 1956; Czechoslovakia, 1968; Afghanistan, 1980), it reacts not at all to operations which go beyond military occupation and entail the annexation of whole provinces (Finnish South Karelia, East Prussia, half of Poland, Ruthenia, Roumanian Bessarabia, etc.) or of countries (Estonia, Latvia, and Lithuania). Such annexations are felt by public opinion to be essential to the security of the Soviet Union. Public opinion, that is to say, in the non-Soviet world, for freedom of speech is not allowed in the annexed areas.

Do the Arabs Refuse to Accept Israel?

There is, of course, above all, an outright refusal to have any truck with Israel. But this is something other than refusal by the Arabs.

More especially, the Western anti-Zionist, who is highly critical of Israel, is perfectly aware that the conflict does not concern him directly. Hence he has to show that his attitude is reasonable by claiming that it is shared by the Arabs, and especially by the Palestinians, thus projecting his own unconscious prejudices or ideological preconceptions on to the Arabs—a form of anti-Arab racial prejudice.

There is one short sentence which for me sums up this way of thinking: "The Arabs could do no other than dream of destroying the State of Israel." This bald statement is made by Maxime Rodinson, a French (Jewish) historian of Islamic affairs and the author of a work the title of which, in itself, is almost a profession of faith.[5] Rodinson is not an anti-Zionist of the wilder kind, and for this very reason his cool statement of belief is likely to command assent, whereas the eructations of

---

[5]*Israël et le Refus arabe* ("Israel and the Arab Refusal"), Seuil, Paris.

which I have given a few examples might induce scepticism. True, this statement might seem incompatible with the warm, almost delirious welcome offered by the Egyptian people to the first Israeli civilians to disembark on Egyptian soil. Let us however, admit for the sake of argument that popular enthusiasm of this kind may wane if negotiations between the two countries fail to make progress. What I wish to stress is that Rodinson's idea of history is typically reactionary, for at least a dozen reasons, to wit:

It is *anti-scientific* in so far as it has been clearly disproved by developments. It is a deliberate attempt by the author to close his eyes to what is happening in Egypt and hence, as a statement about the whole of the Arab world, it is an abusive generalization.

It reveals a *static* outlook. History remains fixed because this is how certain people want it to be. However: "History has a trick of not abiding by the moral, aesthetic and other demands of man" (Rodinson).

It is *pessimistic;* there is nothing we can do about the facts. Notice how often reactionaries of all kinds maintain that the heart of man is intrinsically perverse or that belief in progress is an illusion.

It is *opposed to progress*. It says nothing about possible change, development, challenge to accepted belief, or even revolution. Unless the Arab world is unique in being capable of nothing else but dreaming, in Rodinson's sense of the word.

It is *anti-dialectical*, recognizing the will of one party only, the other being nonexistent or anathematized. In this sense, the assertion is a very poor service rendered to the cause Rodinson seeks to support. All reactionaries, incapable by definition of dialectical thinking, are likely to discover this to their cost.

It is *arbitrary* in that there is no precedent to back it up. Where and when has an obsession or dream had power over history in perpetuity? Unless of course the Middle East is the only part of the world in which facts must at all costs be molded to suit preconceptions.

It is *retrograde* in expecting nothing of conciliation, in denying all possibility of coexistence, and in implying that the course of history is molded only by pig-headed preconceptions. Are Israelis and Arabs really condemned to conflict in perpetuity? Yet the world has in recent years witnessed some spectacular reconciliations between long-standing enemies: France and Germany, the United States and China, Albania and Yugoslavia, India and Pakistan, and perhaps soon Black Africa and the Republic of South Africa.

It is *debasing* for those Rodinson seeks to defend. In underestimating Arab thought as purely negative, it is a slight to the Arab peoples themselves, who are identified with their leaders, most of whom happen to be military men promoted to power by a *coup d'Etat*.

It shows *lack of discrimination* and *contempt for facts* to affirm that contemporary Arab history derives solely from frustration and humiliation and to imply that no importance can be attached to the will of individuals, or to economic, social, political, and human factors. It implies that Arab opinion will forever continue to be dominated by a jingoism whipped up and maintained by certain Arab leaders for their own ends.

It is *irresponsible*. A questionable statement of opinion, several times disproved by events, is presented as the plain truth, and Rodinson seems unworried by its consequences, which are grave. His conception of history would seem to assume that war is inevitable. Here again, we all know what the conservatives have to say: "There'll always be wars." "You can't trust Yids or Wogs." "The only good Hun is a dead one." In this particular instance, we are told what kind of war to expect: a war of destruction, a war of genocide.

Hence this approach presupposes a *teratological* movement of history in which one people is to disappear because this disappearance is implicit in the mission entrusted to another people, the Arabs.

One brief phrase thus gives lapidary expression to a thought open to challenge on every score. The above list of objections is not exclusive, but I close it here.

Confusion begins with the generic term "Arabs." The Armenian Orthodox Archbishop of Jerusalem, a resident of more than forty years' standing, who knows rather more about these problems than Western anti-Zionists, once said to me: "The Arabs, collectively, don't exist. There are Arabs, each with his own way of thinking."

An opinion poll undertaken in Cairo (December 1977) revealed that 90% of Egyptians thought that Israel was "in earnest" in seeking peace; 95% thought that the President's new line towards Israel would influence world public opinion in favour of the Arabs. As regards coexistence between Arabs and Jews in Jerusalem, 88.31% of those questioned thought that some means of living together could be found, while only 3.55% felt that coexistence was impossible.[6]

---

[6]*Le Monde*, Paris, 30 December 1977.

Arab-Islamic Anti-Judaism

On the other hand, statements made by leaders of the PLO and of the rejectionist countries (there is no guarantee, I repeat, that they really represent what the peoples concerned are thinking) suggest that the Jews can expect only one of two things: a tolerant condescension, or absolute intolerance. In no case is it admitted that Jews would be entitled to think or behave as Jews, even outside Israel.

Anti-Zionist totalitarianism is, as we have seen, incapable of dialectical thinking, and hence is unable to draw conclusions from these statements. If we try to do so, the only possible conclusion is that the Jews labour under some sort of historic Curse. Born guilty, their fate is to wander, stateless. The traditional anti-Semites in the Arab world say so openly; contrary to the Western anti-Zionists, they carry their thought to its logical extremes. Here is an extract from a statement by Hassan Khalid, Mufti of the Lebanon, at the fourth conference of the Academy of Islamic Research, Cairo (September 1968):

> The Jews were the most atrocious enemies of Islam and the Moslems in the age of our Prophet. Some various, fruitless and immoral obstacles blocked the way of their Call and thus impeded their movements and restrained them from going ahead easily. The selfishness of their leaders—their conceit, stubbornness, wickedness and megalomania—stood in their way.[7]

To give the Egyptian soldier some stomach for battle during the Yom Kippur War in 1973, the Printed Matter and Publications Department of the Egyptian Arab Republic provided each man with a brochure reproducing various sentences from the Koran, such as: "Cursed were the Children of Israel. Surely ye will find that of all men the most hostile to the Believers were the Jews and Polytheists."

I am reluctant to make such points against Egypt as this was prior to November 1977, although the vestiges of such a mentality cannot have disappeared entirely. What is striking is the spontaneous, overwhelming reaction of the Egyptian people once they could freely speak their minds. The call to slaughter did not emerge from the masses; in Egypt, it was imposed from above, as it still is in the countries of the rejectionist camp.

Jewish anti-Zionists, who nevertheless feel a little uncomfortable about allying

[7] *Arab Theologians on Jews and Israel*, p. 63.

themselves with the forces of genocide, sometimes try to escape the difficulty by asserting that there is no such thing as a Jewish people, or if there is one, it exists "only in the Hitlerian sense of the word" (Maxime Rodinson). Proof? It is enough that the enemies of the Jews say so, and with them, those Jews who, not feeling themselves Jewish, demonstratively hold aloof.

Reactionary and entirely negative, Arab-Islamic anti-Zionism runs counter to the very hopes which a "progressive" ought surely to promote. A real progressive would denounce those Arab dictatorial régimes which divert the justified resentment of the peoples they oppress from revolution by deflecting their hatred towards Israel. Instead, a Kosygin, a Tito, and those who attended a "Euro-Arab" seminar[8] in Paris (14–15 January 1978) did their best to stoke the fires of this hatred, give encouragement to the fire-eating colonels of the Arab world, and undermine the edifice, still precarious, of coexistence. Here, on the other hand, is a real man of the Left unsoiled by any suspicion of sympathy with Zion:

> Today the boundary betweeen anti-Semitism and anti-Zionism is often indistinct. It is clear, too, that the anti-Semitism proclaimed by a good many Arab governments is a veil designed to hide the negligence and corruption of the governing classes, and to divert attention from poverty and unemployment by focussing it on an external foe.[9]

Immediately after the Yom Kippur War of 1973, an Arab journalist wrote:

> Egyptian opinion still believes in the Jew as the enemy of Allah. Egyptian newspapers explain that the word "Israel" is derived from *"isra"* (assassin) and *"el"* (God), whence more fuel for the Holy War. The resulting confusion helps the government in directing the attention of the masses away from politics.[10]

---

[8]"The Paris seminar, then, has as its aims the ends pursued by President Boumediene in the Eastern Arab countries in the course of his journey. It is a first step towards a mobilization of the military strength of the Left in Europe and in the Arab world, to buttress the refusal of countries such as the Soviet Union, Iraq, Syria, Libya, Algeria, South Yemen, etc., to support the process initiated by Sadat. To their great satisfaction, the latter's initiative does not, for the time being, seem to have produced specific, satisfactory results." (Ali Mostofi, *Tribune de Genève*, Geneva, 16 January 1978)
[9]G. Chaliand, *The Palestinian Resistance*, Penguin, London, 1972.
[10]F. D. Attar, *Contact*, Tunis, 25 November–10 December 1975.

How can the anti-Zionist use his influence to ensure that the Arab masses are no longer tricked in this way if he himself is taken in? In the same issue of the Middle Eastern journal just quoted we find a faked photograph of Golda Meir, complete with Hitlerian forelock and moustache. The caption appeals to the world's "free film-makers": "Take your cameras and 'shoot' Israeli neo-fascism and the retrograde, racialist Zionist movement, planted by imperialism in the heart of the Arab world at the expense of the rights of the people of Palestine."

The late Jean Paul Sartre has excellently shown that anti-Semitism is not so much an opinion as an incitement to murder:

> I decline to bestow the term "opinion" on a doctrine directed expressly against individuals, calling for their destruction or denying their rights. The right to the free expression of opinion exists to protect freedom of thought, but not anti-Semitism. Incidentally, anti-Semitism derives not from thought but from fear of oneself and of truth . . . . In a word, anti-Semitism is fear of being alive.[11]

These words exactly apply to extreme anti-Zionism. This kind of anti-Zionism is no mere speculation, but a weapon in the total war it is designed to bring about. It gives encouragement, and supplies arguments, to one of the parties in the dispute, so that the party in question may buckle down to its work of destroying the other with a clear conscience. Conversely, anti-Zionists try to weaken the defences of that other party by spreading alarm, despondency and self-questioning in its ranks. This work of undermining morale also extends to those who, like the President of Egypt and his people, prefer to play the card of peace.

Those Arab anti-Zionists who swear that they are not anti-Jewish make little effort to show in what respect their views differ from classical anti-Semitism. Shukeiri, the loud-mouthed Arab spokesman before the 1967 war, was put out to grass only because he had been lamentably unsuccessful. His appeals for recourse to fire and sword against the Jews have been replaced by slogans designed to hoodwink the naive or the prejudiced in the West—slogans such as that calling for the institution of a "secular, democratic State" in Palestine.[12] But if we run through the pro-PLO press, we shall find the same old themes, even the same

---

[11] J. P. Sartre, *Anti-Semite and Jew*, Schocken Books, New York, 1966.
[12] See the chapter on this in Y. Harkabi, *op. cit.*

quotations from the bogus *Protocols of the Elders of Zion*. Edouard Saab (later killed in Beirut by an Arab bullet) wrote in a Lebanese paper:

> Rather than invoking the Apocalypse, it might be better to mention the *Protocols of the Elders of Zion*. It may well be, as some assert, that this work is bogus, the work of some horrid Nazi. But is not this the document which depicts a monster with tentacles ready for any foul deed provided Zion lives and prospers?[13]

Some people, such as Professor Benachenhou, writing in an Algerian official organ, can even invoke the *Protocols* while protesting that they are not in any way anti-Jewish: "The Jews aim at world domination. Full of their racial superiority, they have always been convinced that they alone have the ability to direct the world's affairs."[14] Accused of anti-Jewish prejudice in a French newspaper,[15] he disclaims the allegation. It is not without interest to observe how he does so. In a letter to the editor, he recalls that in a professional association he had voted for a Jewish writer: ". . . incidentally, a charming man, highly cultured, well-bred; just to show you how tolerant Algerians are." He goes on to make himself clear: "I simply listed the points set forth in the *Protocols*, indicating how dangerous it would be to give effect to the Zionist platform, as adopted by the aggressive, expansionist State of Israel." One might be forgiven for wondering how tolerant he would have been had his protégé been less charming, cultured, or well-bred.

To measure the full decline of standards in Algeria, it is sufficient to go back to the recent past. When for the first time I had the honour of meeting Ferhat Abbas, then President of the Provisional Government of the Algerian Republic (in Montreux, Switzerland, 1958), he came to welcome me at the door—not knowing who I was—and addressed me as he would have addressed any friendly visitor from France, beginning (and in the middle of a war of independence he must have had other things to worry about) by saying how indignant he had been on learning that "Death to the Jews!" was being scribbled on walls in Paris. Such a phenomenon, he thought, was of a nature seriously to affect his opinion of France.

[13]*L'Orient—Le Jour*, Beirut, Lebanon, 8 January 1974.
[14]*Algérie-Actualités*, Algiers, April 1970.
[15]*Le Monde*, Paris, 7 April 1970.

Today, the anti-Jewish campaign launched by the more extreme Arab governments is accompanied by an attempt to induce the West to believe that Jews in the Arab countries are perfectly satisfied with their lot. In the Arab world, we are told, there can be no anti-Semitic feeling, since the Arabs are Semites themselves. In fact, this is playing on words; there still exists in the Moslem world a suspicion of the Unbelievers, sometimes dormant, sometimes finding expression in hysterical outbursts—a suspicion which many Moslem leaders play on for their own ends by invoking the Koran, in an attempt to justify Moslem colonialism and expansionism. It is dishonest, and just another attempt to shift responsibility to Israel, to say that recent excesses have no roots in traditional Islamic teaching.

Let it not be imagined that only a few dictators have been infected by the anti-Jewish virus, and that the *fedayeen*, automatically classified as progressive,[16] have been successful in avoiding it. At an interview with a sheikh, arranged for him by the Fatah movement, Chaliand confesses that he could hardly believe his ears when told by that dignitary that the Jews had tried to kill Mohammed. The same author found the following on a series of postcards issued by Fatah: "The atrocities performed by the Jews on the Canaanites find a historical parallel only in what they did to the Arabs in 1948."[17]

The Right Kind of Jew and the Horrid Zionists

We may therefore dismiss the quibble whereby our adversaries, while disclaiming any objection to Jews as such, claim only to oppose the Zionists and the "Zionist entity"—i.e., Israel.

Under the dictatorship of the Kremlin, an anti-Jewish campaign of the most traditional kind can be subsumed under the official campaign against Zionism. Sometimes there is no attempt at disguise. A widely read Russian literary review quotes a certain Dr. Malashko, a historian, who denounces "the Jewish bourgeoisie, which has become a dominant caste in capitalist society," specifying that this bourgeoisie has "appropriated a considerable proportion of the world's wealth and is trying to lay hands on what is left." Malashko is quoted as saying that: "The Zionists promote those who are useful to them, while often placing insurmountable obstacles in the path of talented people not lucky enough to be Jewish."

[16] In reporting events in the Lebanon, the French press is particularly fond of referring to the "Palestinian-progressive" faction.
[17] G. Chaliand, *op. cit.*

further: "Zionist ideology derives from Judaic dogma, dividing mankind into two unequal parts: the Jews, who are the children of God, and the non-Jews, whom the Jews despise. Clearly, so wicked a doctrine is bound to produce suspicion, if not hostility, among people able to think for themselves." The author of this article, one Dmitri Zhoukov, well-known as a pathological hater of Jews, having thus justified Czarist pogroms, "finds it curious that Hitler, having invoked German racial superiority, should have borrowed Zionist language"—but this is hardly surprising, "since modern authors have clearly revealed the links between Zionism and fascism in their common hatred of the Soviet Union. Moreover, their views on race are substantially the same."[18]

Arguments for murder encourage further killings. The apologists for the pogroms, whether they mean to or not, are encouraging modern versions of the same crimes and justifying those who, as a legitimate reason for mowing down the innocent and desecrating their dead bodies, brand their victims as "Zionists." Observe that the Jews expelled from Poland in the late 1960s (some of them had been victims of Munich) had become "Zionists" despite themselves, having remained in Poland (the real Zionists had left long before) precisely because they were not Zionists; some of them were even unaware that they were Jews. It would be difficult to imagine a better argument for Zionism than this.

Hence a whole nation, and any of its citizens at random, are condemned to disappear. There is no precedent for this in modern history. Did even the fiercest enemies of United States policies in Vietnam ever open fire at random, with submachine guns, in Kennedy Airport or within the precincts of a New York nursery school? Has there ever been an incident in which some ferociously anti-communist group has gunned down Soviet tourists (denounced as "Stalinists")? No, and had such things occurred, those responsible would have been denounced as mad and bad. Not so when Israel is concerned.

Anti-Zionism carried to such a pitch is in fact *madness*. Israeli Jews are killed because they proclaim themselves as such. Israel is to be destroyed because it is a Jewish State. Incidentally, the hostage-taking is never designed to improve the lot of the Palestinian masses, but rather to obtain the release of other killers, previously detained, for further feats. At Munich (5–6 September 1972) and Entebbe (4–5 July 1976), the aim was to secure the release of the Japanese terrorist who had survived the Lod massacre (30 May 1972).

It is well known (although there is reluctance to draw the necessary conclusions)

---

[18]*Moskva*, Moscow, March 1975, p. 221.

that the Palestinian "freedom fighters" in Khartoum (March 1973) displayed particular brutality towards one hostage—a Belgian diplomat—mistaken for a Jew. Acknowledgment of a "mistake" should not lead to condonement. Obviously, the pro-Palestinian assassins at Lod had nothing against the Puerto Rican Catholics they mowed down "by mistake." What they wanted was to fill Jewish bodies with lead, to watch Jewish blood flow. Obviously, the bomb which exploded on 3 October 1980 outside a Paris synagogue was designed to kill some scores of people leaving the building and not "innocent Frenchmen who happened to be crossing the street" (a revealing *lapsus linguae* by the French Prime Minister, Raymond Barre). The murderers, with the men, the movements and the governments which inspire, support and approve them, are obsessed with the destruction of a nation and blind to anything else. Hitler was mad in the same sense; fortunately, his modern disciples wield less power.

The same holds good of the massacres at the airports in Athens (5 August 1973) and Rome (17 August 1973). At Athens, it was an "honest slip"[19]—the *fedayeen*, anxious to strike at Jewish emigrants bound for Israel, simply opened fire on people standing in the wrong line. In Rome, a check by the Italian authorities took the *fedayeen* by surprise; they opened fire at once, at random, regardless of their possible victims. The fact that most of those killed and wounded were not Jews makes the crime, if anything, even worse. As always when motives are totally irrational and the target is a bogey, violence knows neither bounds nor scruples. A locked door is forced open; should it fail to yield, then the neighbour's door will do instead. The point is at all costs to take life.

Naturally, one can have too much of a good thing; in an Israeli village, the assassins have on occasion shot down other Arabs, mistaking them for Jews. In apology to a little girl whose parents have just been killed: "We didn't know." They had knocked on the wrong door. Coldly, the Western press reports that Moslems have been killed in error, and error, of course, is no crime.

Perhaps we may exculpate as "error" what happens when fools in good faith are taken in. In German-occupied France, there were good "socialists" and excellent "Europeans," sincere believers in the collaboration preached by the French pro-German press, who in 1945 were surprised to find that they were expected to justify themselves; in fact, most of them were treated with indulgence, as inveterate political innocents. The fact remains that they had closed their eyes to calls for

---

[19] In 1968, a French Minister described the Russian occupation of Czechoslovakia as an *"accident de parcours"*—just one of those things that happen, morally neutral, a bona fide mistake.

murder, and apologies for crime, published in that same press. Those who today eagerly collaborate with the Palestinian "revolution" may be blind in the same way. But when no less a person than the French Minister for Foreign Affairs, having shaken hands with the chief of the PLO, goes out of his way to describe this man as "reasonable and moderate," we may legitimately suspect cynicism rather than credulity, especially when he adds: "The PLO ought to forgo terrorism." How simple it all is! Colonialists ought not to oppress the colonized; racialists ought not to practice *apartheid*. Let us encourage them in the right direction by describing them as reasonable and moderate.

The fate the potential victims may expect is no different from that which awaited them at the time of mass destruction, even if accompanied by casuistry. Let us accept the latter for what it is worth, even though, from time to time, the cat is let out of the bag.[20]

So, at Munich and Entebbe, the Jews as such were not the target? Fair enough; the victims were not the ordinary kind of Jew, citizens of States liable to persecute or protect them as circumstances or political convenience might dictate. Although weaponless, they represented something to be feared—Jews with a country of their own, Jews disinclined to accept a "democratic, secular State of Palestine" which they know would not hesitate a moment in reducing them to stateless cyphers. Dub a Jew "Zionist" and any crime can be committed against him with the clearest of consciences.

This convenient confusion between anti-Zionism and anti-Semitism is nothing new. A similar cynicism, and similar sneers, were in order during the great Stalinist show-trials, conducted in Prague, among other places. The survivors have described how, arrested as Jews, they were addressed as "Zionists" so that the interrogators could feign to be anti-Zionist rather than anti-Jewish, while insulting their victims with taunts traditionally reserved for Jews, thus giving brutal bad manners a Marxist dimension hitherto lacking. I quote at random:

> Every limb aches, after innumerable calls to stand to attention, after several days of blows (my head being the chief target for the interrogator's heavy fist) as a punishment for "Jewish stubbornness." My head feels as though it were going to split into a thousand pieces.[21]

---

[20] A spokesman for the Algerian Embassy in London, after Dr. Kissinger's appointment as President Nixon's plenipotentiary: "We make no distinction between Jew and Israeli."
[21] Mordekhai Oren, *Prisonnier politique à Prague*, Julliard, Paris.

Or consider the following questions and answers:

"Would you be ready to confess that in 1948, after Tito's betrayal, you met Moshe Pijade as well as Dr. Bebler in Belgrade?"
"I didn't meet Pijade in 1948, and even if I had, that would have been no crime. Nor was it a crime to meet Bebler."
"He's a Jew, and you too, and both of you are Zionists."[22]

Maxime Rodinson considers that Oren, treated as described above, stands "revealed for what he was during the Prague trials"—i.e., as "one of a band of traitors, saboteurs and agents of the Anglo-American secret services who found therein [i.e., in an Israeli left-wing party, J.G.] a ready-made camouflage for their nefarious activities."[23]

To quote Artur London:

On the third day of my arrest, I found myself confronted with four men in uniform and a civilian wearing Party insignia, who said: "Not all of what Hitler did was good, but at least he did one good thing in destroying the Jews. He didn't do so entirely, but we shall finish the job."[24]

Even today, those who regret that there were loopholes in the Final Solution are active, as proved by the following extract from the Egyptian extremist press: "Heading of a letter from a reader in Alexandria: 'Beware of the Daughters of Zion!' " The letter ran thus:

It is strange that Moslem Egypt should welcome Israeli girls as tourists. They come, not to admire an idolatrous Pharaonic culture, but to destroy Islamic values. The Jews are very good at this, as they have proved in the United States, France, Italy, Belgium and Scandinavia . . . , countries morally defiled by Jewry.[25]

Assasination is justified in advance by rendering its victims less than human. For this purpose they are given an odious label; for what is "Zionist" but a label

[22]Ibid.
[23]La Nouvelle Critique, Paris, February 1953.
[24]Le Nouvel Observateur, Paris, 6–12 January 1969.
[25]Le Monde, Paris, 11 October 1980.

invested with an aura of dishonour? The German National Socialists proceeded in like manner with those they were determined to destroy.

Assassins as Allies of the KGB

What can be said about these outrages against Jewish flesh and blood, especially those directed against children? How can indignation, beyond a certain point, be expressed? It may be absurd to feel, or to attempt to express, such emotions at a time when they are no longer fashionable and when left-wing intellectuals (who have only very rarely and incompletely taken responsibility for action) laud as "revolutionary exploits" the taking and murder of hostages. The very same persons who exulted when "Zionist" blood was shed were active from October 1977 in the Western European capitals in support of the Baader-Meinhof gang and its Palestinian friends and disciples, notably after the Palma-Mogadiscio hijacking, in the course of which eighty-six entirely innocent hostages ceased to be innocent after the hijackers had decided to consider them "filthy Jews" and maltreated them as such, murdering the captain of the aircraft, who had tried to save his passengers (he was a Frenchman—not that his murder had the slightest effect on the pro-Arab stance of the Paris government).[26]

Those intellectuals who at a safe distance support indiscriminate slaughter would seem to be at one with the Ayatollah Khomeini, reported to have praised the infliction of death as a "sacred ideal." Certainly, what they are admiring is something entirely foreign to the European liberal tradition. The Spanish nationalist General Millán Astray, with his call *"Viva la muerte!"* was not in the past much admired by the kind of people who today support the PLO.

True, more people have been killed recently in Uganda, Argentina, Chile, Cambodia or Equatorial Guinea, and wherever barbarians have taken power. But there is little point in comparing the relative capacities of common graves. What is frightening is that there is no common language between victims and assassins, whether the latter be black or red, official or clandestine. We have nothing to say which will bridge the gap. To try to argue is like trying to reason with the Van-

---

[26]The "revolutionary" Palestinian hijackers, running berserk, behaved thus: "The head pirate called out the names of three girls who were Jewish. He said they would be executed in the morning. . . . They found a Jewish sign on the co-pilot's watch and made us swear we would never buy anything Jewish again." (*International Herald Tribune*, 20 October 1977)

dals busy with the sack of Rome by urging that their depredations run counter to Roman law. Words of rage and indignation, shouted in the face of the storm, are simply carried away. All we can do is to highlight abuse of language and show ourselves capable of making a proper use of the political vocabulary our opponents employ.

From the political point of view, the activities of the *fedayeen* and the grave moral responsibilities of those who support them are very different from what these supporters claim or imagine. There is not much to be gained by following the official Israeli line and describing the *fedayeen* as "murderers"; they themselves are proud to be so called. What has to be stressed is that their crimes cannot be put on the same level as those committed, for instance, by the Catholic opponents of the *status quo* in Northern Ireland (I deliberately choose an area where passions run high). Whatever judgment we may pass on the crimes committed by this minority, and whether or not they help in bringing about the proclaimed aim of Irish unity, those responsible for such acts have never in their wildest dreams thought of invading England and destroying England as a nation. The avowed aim of the PLO, on the other hand, as constantly reaffirmed, is the destruction of Israel, and in so far as this is so, the PLO is an instrument of pan-Arab imperialism. The assassins here are "colonialist" assassins. In so far as they claim to act on behalf of a "revolution" or of a "secular State," they are imposters. And in so far as they call for, encourage, and support the oppression of Jews in a police state—the Soviet Union—they are acting in the interests of that country and as allies of the KGB.

On 28 September 1973, near Marchegg, on the Austro-Czechoslovak border, a Palestinian commando group attacked a train full of Soviet Jews on their way to Israel. This was a first-class success, if oppression of Jews be the criterion. A Lebanese newspaper quite rightly observed that "the *fedayeen* have obtained results for which the Arab countries have striven in vain for months." So brilliant an exploit—Chancellor Kreisky was forced to accede to the Palestinian demands—could not but encourage others. Even Hitler did not manage (indeed, he probably never tried) to prevent neutral countries, even those encircled by his forces, like Switzerland, from granting asylum to Jewish or other fugitives. Today, it suffices to seize fresh hostages to obtain the immediate release of persons convicted of previous hostage-taking, and so on indefinitely. In many countries "Zionist" blood can thus be shed with impunity. Not only this; the policies of sovereign States can be modified, and even reversed, by terror.

There was no hope of an end to the process as long as sovereign States, in yielding to blackmail (compare press condemnations of Israeli "intransigence" as against the "firmness" of Arab States, the difference in vocabulary not being in favour of Israel), were guilty of breaches of international law. For the Geneva Conventions, the only international instrument valid in this field, forbid surrender to blackmail following the taking of hostages, and not only the taking of hostages.[27] The reasons for this prohibition are clear enough in the light of recent painful experience; once a breach of the law is officially accepted, the very foundations of law are liable to crumble, especially when they are none too secure already. The result is the law of the jungle. The rescue operation at Entebbe (July 1976) was to some extent successful in arresting this process, in so far, at any rate, as it was imitated at Mogadiscio in October 1977.

The motives of those who take Jewish hostages, and of the governments which encourage, arm, and applaud the hostage-takers, are evident enough. "The aim is at all costs to prevent the emigration of Soviet Zionists," one of those involved in the Marchegg feat has said. He added: "Any Jew wishing to leave the Soviet Union is *ipso facto* a Zionist." There could be no better way of proclaiming that Zionism is a movement of Jewish emancipation, to be resisted at all costs. For these people and for these governments, denial of Jewish emancipation is a historical achievement, beneficial in itself and, it is to be hoped, definitive. Here anti-Zionism becomes less and less distinguishable from anti-Semitism; the Jew is to be pursued and thwarted as soon as he tries to free himself from what (in the Soviet Union at any rate) is repression of the colonial type. Those who support policies of this kind are perfectly consistent in claiming that the very existence of Israel is an aggression.[28] While Egyptian policy has, fortunately, evolved, the policy of the PLO has not. When a so-called national liberation movement thus becomes an agent of oppression, independently of the cause it was originally founded to defend, it becomes as obnoxious as was the Sudeten German Front of 1938—the movement, championed by Hitler, of the Bohemian German minority in Czechoslovakia. It is false to claim that there is nothing else the PLO can do; it has deliber-

---

[27]Statement by Marcel Naville, President of the International Committee of the Red Cross, *International Review of the Red Cross*, Geneva, October 1971.
[28]Abdul Nasser, Cairo, 28 May 1967, at a press conference. The date is significant, immediately before the Six-Day War.

ately reverted to barbarism in its campaign against the Jewish people so as radically to compromise any hope of coexistence in the Holy Land.

It is sometimes said that terrorism is the poor man's, the underdog's, way of waging war. In 1962, however, the OAS (a right-wing movement among the French settler population of Algeria opposed to any concession to Arab nationalism) claimed that it could defend its interests only by terror. Colonel Qaddafi, champion of Palestinian terrorism in its most extreme form, is not as far as I know especially poor. Are we to believe that if the PLO could lay its hands on better and more murderous weapons, it would refrain from using them?

A Political Comparison

Perhaps Jewish ("Zionist") boys and girls have to be massacred as a prelude to the harmonious coexistence of "Jews, Christians, and Moslems in a democratic, secular Palestine"? It is certainly true that Hitler's propaganda machine went to no such trouble in justifying his policies or rendering them more acceptable.

In comparing the men and methods of today with those of Hitler's time, there are, I know, comparisons which cause tempers to rise and hence must be handled with care. The day after Maalot, the French newspaper *Le Monde* wrote in an editorial that the "odious blackmail practised by the Palestinian terrorists was worthy of the worst Nazi crimes."[29] A few days later, in a dispute with the Embassy of Israel, the comparison was made again.[30] A judgment such as this, by the most respected of French newspapers, not generally noted for any pro-Israel sympathies, carries weight.

If, then, there are persons who behave like Nazis, they should be treated as such and rejected by the international community, not released whenever their accomplices threaten another outrage, and not recognized by international organizations as representatives of a "national liberation movement" thanks to the maneuvers of a handful of potentates whose power depends on their oil and their legitimacy on the blood they have shed. Nor is there any call for the Minister of Foreign Affairs of a country (France) once noted for its sense of moderation and measure to go out of his way to describe the leader of this movement as "reasonable, moderate and statesmanlike."

[29]*Le Monde*, Paris, 16 May 1974.
[30]*Ibid.*, 28 May 1974.

As I have said, it is difficult enough to find words to convey adequate indignation; however, I remember writing the following in a poem called "Fright" (1942):

> We say to ourselves:
> They just can't do that.
> Or else:
> They are capable of anything.

I was thinking of those who at that time were all set to destroy us, little imagining that less than forty years later I should have occasion to feel the same emotions.

There is, however, one fairly important difference between National Socialist Germans and *fedayeen*. The reign of the Nazis was cold, cruel, Wagnerian, and mysterious in certain ways, as befits a tragedy. Of humour there was never the slightest sign. Our enemies of today are given to joking, although others may not find the jokes in the best of taste. For instance, after the Maalot killings, the editor of a Lebanese newspaper wrote: "After all, these children might have been, not hostages, but witnesses to negotiations which the government of Israel obstinately refuses." In this way, odious blackmail is at least enlivened by a spice of fancy, totally inconceivable under Hitler.

An Egyptian journalist, Lutfallah Soliman, finds it reprehensible that certain people "should still claim" that the innocents killed at Maalot were "children between twelve and fourteen years of age."[31] They had, he assures us, been "between fifteen and seventeen years old." One imagines the terrorists (I normally eschew this word but use it deliberately here, since they set out to terrify the hostages before killing them and to intimidate Israel in so doing) asking each boy and girl for his or her birth certificate and sending back to their parents those too young to be put down, as though a year more or less in the victim's age would justify the crime. At dawn, as their compatriots had done at Kiryat Shemona, these young Arabs had killed infants in their cradles, just to get their hands in, no doubt, and with no intention of using their victims as hostages (or "witnesses"). Soliman may sleep more easily of nights in the thought that these innocent victims were adolescents rather than children, but the killers themselves deliberately sought out the very youngest children, knowing that in killing them they would inflict the most grievous possible wound on Israel, in body and in spirit.

[31]*Ibid.*, 8 June 1974.

This is why the crime is unforgivable, irreparable; not merely because no code of ethics—be it traditional, liberal, or "revolutionary"—can accept it, but because the criminals themselves wished it to be so as a matter of policy.

Soliman feels that "nevertheless, an attempt should be made to get to the bottom of things." He observes that "Israelis, Egyptians, Syrians and Jordanians can make war and negotiate a cease-fire" and wonders: "What can the Palestinians do to get negotiations started with a view to the release of their kith and kin?" Has Soliman, a champion of what he calls the Palestinian "non-beings," ever heard of the fate of the Jews in the Soviet Union, Iraq, and Syria, who, much as they would like to do so, cannot negotiate their own release? He must at least be familiar with the word "ghetto," today all too loosely used. At the time he was pondering these matters, the term still bore its original sense at Haret el Yahud, a district in Damascus in which the Jews subsist as real "non-beings" unable to leave or to communicate with the outside world. Latterly, there has been some slight evidence of an improvement in their lot. They nevertheless remain hostages to the current dictator of Syria. What would Soliman have to say if some of these Syrian Jews, having managed to escape, were to make hostages of his children so as to be able to negotiate the release of their own?

I shall not dwell on the tragic confusion manifest on that day within the government of Israel. The responsibility remains squarely with those who had put it in a position such that any decision was potentially fraught with tragic consequences. Exactly as with gangsters who by force entangle you in some sinister affair and then offer you a way out: you can if you like refuse, but only if you are prepared to risk your life. When what is at stake is not a single life but the lives of a hundred children, then confusion and bewilderment among those who have to decide become, to say the least, understandable. In so far as individual members of the government refused to yield to blackmail, in accordance with the tough line taken by the government in previous cases, they were doing something to frustrate attempts which might be made anywhere in the world to use children as counters in blackmail. In attempting, by a desperate decision, to stop the spread of terrorism, they were protecting all children, everywhere.

In December 1975, some twenty children were made hostages by South Moluccan rebels at the Indonesian Consulate-General in Amsterdam. Such things had been unknown before the *fedayeen* led the way. The only possible means of nipping blackmail in the bud is to do as Israel has done and refuse to yield, no matter how much courage it may take to do so. To yield may seem easier, but the canker will spread. French children were kidnapped in Djibouti (February 1976) and the South Moluccans took further hostages in May 1977 and March 1978. One good thing, however, has emerged: the public is now aware that there is a South Moluccan problem, i.e., that the Third World has its own colonial troubles to hide, and that the oppressed, unlike the PLO, are not themselves potential oppressors. They claim national independence, not the end of any other country as an independent entity.

Unfortunately, we cannot "get to the bottom of things," as Soliman would have us do, without mentioning the responsibility borne by Western pro-Palestinians for the sufferings of Israeli children. When we read, in a self-styled "Trotskyist" paper published in France, that one particular Palestinian movement is more "moderate" than the others in that it would—to begin with—agree to the creation of a Palestinian State limited to Gaza and the West Bank, and is therefore guilty of betraying the Palestinian cause, we may well wonder what prompted the writing of those lines: unconscious anti-Jewish prejudice which the author was ashamed to confess, or frustration at being cheated of his "revolution"? "Objectively" (to use Marxist jargon) these supporters are just as guilty as those they urge to destroy a nation and its children. It is a tragic paradox (there are many of them in history) that this movement, accused of betraying the cause by its moderation, boasts of the Maalot killings. The Western champions of other people's revolutions, although ideologically naive, are criminally responsible.

To close the file, let us quote Nayef Hawatmeh, head of the movement referred to above: "The Jew, with his reactionary culture and institutions . . ." At that time he had not forfeited the confidence of European Trotskyists; he still, however, enjoys that of other "progressives." The latter, in their entirety, place their confidence in Yasser Arafat, head of the PLO, whose utterances we are told (not without condescension) "have to be interpreted"; we have to read between the lines. Perhaps I may be pardoned for attaching less importance to words (and even less to what I am told is tacitly implied) than to deeds, and especially to deeds of blood of which the PLO boasts.

"Worthy of the worst Nazi crimes." I come back to these words, the implications of which take us beyond these deeds and those who encouraged their commission. If piracy, hostage-taking and murder are not stopped, it will be a judgment of history on an epoch which is destroying the kind of world we lived for, i.e., the world which Nazi paganism opposed. A world in which "justice and charity would go hand-in-hand" (A. Camus). A world denigrated by certain circles in the

West on the grounds that it is the fruit of an obsolete Western culture, overlooking the fact that this is the world in which the peoples oppressed by Moscow, Baghdad, Lagos and Djakarta place their hopes.

The killers of yesterday and today, by the crimes they commit and the ends they pursue, are opening the door to a very different and much more sinister world, based on blood lust, human sacrifice (other people's lives for preference), a taste for violence justified by some new international order, then gradually degenerating into a value in itself, requiring no justification. It will come as no surprise to find a French writer who revels in self-abasement (by theft or treachery or by the admiration he feels for the thug) expressing himself thus: "The French Gestapo demanded two fascinating things: treachery and theft."[32] It is entirely in keeping with his character that this man should carry a rabid hatred of Israel to the point of defending the killers of Maalot.[33]

I write these lines not only in defence of Jewish infant martyrs, whether cremated by the Germans or defenestrated by Arab "freedom fighters." I am thinking of other children, too, small Palestinians, their faces ugly with hatred, as shown on propaganda photographs. Their big brothers are criminal not only for massacring small Israelis, but also for teaching small Arabs to hate and for stifling in them any faith in human nature. One of the most frightening things in the world today (and God knows there are other horrors) is to behold these children clutching weapons and to contemplate the expressions on their faces.

I hope I am right in believing that the criminals who have trained these children to hate will be unsuccessful in deceiving everybody all the time. We simply have to believe that these children are not irrevocably lost for the cause of peace and coexistence.

---

[32] Jean Genêt, A *Thief's Journal*, Olympia Press, Paris, 1954.
[33] See T. Ben Jelloun, "Jean Genêt avec les Palestiniens", in *Le Monde diplomatique*, Paris, July 1974.

V
Targets Missed

For Israel's enemies, verdict and indictment are simultaneous and replace both judicial inquiry and the cross-questioning of witnesses. For the killers they employ, the execution precedes all else. The Israelis rarely refuse (and indeed have no need to refuse) a full, impartial inquiry, knowing as they do that if the matter at issue were to be judged on points of fact or law their case would usually be upheld. But they have to realize that their enemies are determined to avoid such an inquiry, as incompatible with their own one-sided view of the reality of facts and the validity of law. This is apparent from the attacks launched with unparalleled tenacity against the Jewish State within what is commonly known as the "United Nations system."

The United Nations—United Against Whom?

The principal merit of the system, with its world-wide coverage, is perhaps that it exists, and by existing fills a gap, offering a brake and a safety-valve for the forces of international dissension. The trouble is that, modelled as it is on the parliamentary assemblies of the democratic countries, the system has allowed itself to be dominated by a group of states with neither democratic traditions nor respect for democratic procedures. These countries abuse the freedoms offered them by the system (freedoms which, internally, they do not recognize) to impose the will of an unprincipled and opportunistic majority. Within this system the Jewish State has constantly been treated as individual Jews so often were during the twenty centuries of the dispersion. Unable, so far, to destroy this State by more direct and expeditious means, a number of countries, spurred on by the Soviet Union, Iraq, Iran, Syria, and other worthy defenders of human rights, have joined hands in an effort to denigrate and injure Israel by all possible means. Thus it is that year after year, from every rostrum, at every level, on every conceivable occasion, a systematic, vicious, remorseless campaign is waged against one country only — Israel. Certain United Nations meetings, held in theory to discuss and settle urgent international problems, spend more time in condemning Israel than on all their other agenda items put together. The ritual is performed with the more fervour in that if offers a splendid means of distracting attention from the skeletons to be found in so many national cupboards. No other nation is treated in this way. However vehement in tone, no United Nations document concerning the Republic of South Africa (another favourite target) goes beyond a condemnation (justifiable) of *apartheid*; none call in question the very existence of that country.

Of course, one more condemnation of Israel by the United Nations is not all that tragic; no blood is shed. But its effects on ways of thinking, behaviour and policy cannot be overlooked. And it may lead to deeds. For moral denigration encourages physical elimination; a few days after the adoption of the resolution of 10 November 1975 challenging the very existence of Israel, a bomb killed six young people (all of them refugees from Arab countries) in Jerusalem. The PLO forthwith claimed the credit for this feat and, justifying it by reference to the United Nations resolution, described it as "heroic."

It might have been hoped that after President Sadat's gesture the diplomacy of Egypt would change direction, or at least adopt a different tone. Not at all, unfortunately. The world did not have long to wait; on 3 December 1977, the United Nations General Assembly once more adopted a string of anti-Israeli resolutions, with Egypt following the general movement. One of them set up a special international body to concern itself with "anti-Zionist propaganda." On 10 February 1978, nine countries (including Egypt) countersigned and secured the adoption (France abstaining) by the United Nations Human Rights Commission in Geneva of a resolution more strident than ever, in which Israel was mentioned only to be qualified as an "affront" to mankind. The resolution affirmed the "inalienable right of the Palestinian people to self-determination without interference from outside" and called for "the establishment of a fully independent sovereign State of Palestine." It reaffirmed "the inalienable right of the Palestinians to return to their homes and property, from which they had been driven," demanding that those returning should enjoy a right to self-determination. It recognized "the right of the Palestinians to recover their rights by all possible means" and went so far as to "call upon all States and international organizations to assist the Palestinian people through its representative, the Palestinian Liberation Organization." At a press conference held afterwards, the PLO representative expressed his satisfaction at "an unprecedented international victory." He may have been right; on 11 March 1978, one month after this resolution had been adopted, a PLO ambush on the Tel Aviv–Haifa road killed thirty-seven people and injured eighty-two others, many of them children. Once more, this slaughter was greeted as "heroic" by the very organization which the United Nations had called on all countries to assist. This, like other grisly deeds, was inspired by the U.N. resolution adopted on 10 November 1975, the master text by reference to which condemnations of, and imprecations against, Israel are justified.

It might be illuminating, for the purposes of comparison, to take a look at what was going on in the rest of the world on that particular date.

A Day Like Any Other

Let us take any major newspaper reporting the events of this day; for instance, *Le Monde* for 12 November 1975 (the *International Herald Tribune* would do as well).

In Africa, "two republics clash over Angola": on the one hand, the People's Republic of the MPLA, backed by the USSR; on the other, the People's Democratic Republic, for which the FNLA and UNITA (backed by Zaire) are setting up a joint "Revolutionary Council." Later, the more consistently backed of the two bodies will win, obtaining exclusive recognition (including recognition by Zaire) and exclusive admission to the United Nations (where it will duly vote against Israel); *ipso facto*, this government will be the only one entitled to claim that it is "revolutionary," "popular," and "democratic." In the vote on Zionism, Zaire will abstain. Out of prudence, perhaps; who knows? We observe with interest another, more significant abstention—that of the United Nations as a whole, which refuses to take cognizance of the war raging in Angola.

That November was marked by other wars as well: "A rough estimate of deaths due to clashes in the Lebanon is that some seven thousand men have lost their lives, not counting civilians." The following year there will be far more, notably among the Palestinians, but the United Nations will remain indifferent. On 10 November 1975, Lebanon voted in favour of the anti-Zionist resolution.

In Spain, where General Franco's death is expected at any moment, there is "a fresh wave of arrests among the ranks of the extreme Left." In Manhattan, on the day when the anti-Zionist resolution is put to the vote, the representative of Spain is absent. An oversight? Perhaps. One thing is certain, namely, that like everybody else he had conveniently forgotten General Assembly Resolution No. 31 (12 December 1946), adopted when the United Nations had only just come into existence, which "condemned the Franco régime in Spain and decided that, as long as that régime remains, Spain may not be admitted to the United Nations." This resolution was based on Security Council Documents S/75 and S/76, according to which "incontrovertible documentary evidence established that Franco was a guilty party with Hitler and Mussolini in the conspiracy to wage war against those countries which eventually in the course of the world war became banded together as the United Nations." Perhaps that resolution had been just a slip, excusable on the grounds of youth.

From the other side of Europe, *Le Monde* refers to the case of Anatoli Marchenko, a thirty nine-year-old Soviet writer who has already spent nine years in prison and has been again condemned to four years' exile at Choona, in Siberia, for disobeying restrictions on his place of residence. According to his wife, half the population of Choona is made up of "Russian, Ukrainian, Latvian and Lithuanian exiles and former prisoners." Neither Latvia nor Lithuania, of course, has a vote in the United Nations, not even being represented, and it is conveniently forgotten that these two Baltic states, together with Estonia (all of them independent between the two world wars), were on 17 June 1940 annexed by the Soviet Union, then occupied by the Germans, then re-annexed by the U.S.S.R. On the other hand, the Ukraine, like Byelorussia, is a full member of the United Nations, although in fact no more independent than Arizona, Brittany or Wales. This, of course, is the outcome of an arrangement whereby the Soviet Union enjoys three votes instead of one. Naturally, on 10 November 1975, all three votes will be cast against Israel.

On that day, the new masters of Bangladesh, having murdered the father of the nation, Mujibur Rahman, and his family, make numerous arrests, after which "the President of the Republic and the heads of the three armed services are sharing power." In the United Nations, where *coups d'Etat* interest nobody, Bangladesh joins hands with the countries of the Arab and Soviet blocs (and, irony of history! with India and Pakistan) in condemning Zionism. (This second President was to endure a similar fate on 30 May, 1981, the United Nations remaining equally unperturbed.)

To close this brief survey (which overlooks the numerous peoples persecuted or in revolt; they are referred to only incidentally, as part of some local news item—for instance, the 35 million aborigines maltreated by the Delhi government[1]), let us turn to the next page of our newspaper. Under the heading "Decolonization in the Western Sahara," we read that participants in the Moroccan "Green March" (designed to demonstrate Moroccan claims to the Spanish Sahara) are retreating to wherever they had set out from, while "Spanish military sources claim that the Frente Polisario [the Saharan independence movement] is supported by the people of the Spanish Sahara" and that "negotiations have begun for a peaceful settlement between Madrid and Rabat." Later, Morocco and Mauritania, neocolonialist countries, were to absorb this territory without objection from the United Nations. In the meantime, both countries take the view that "Zionism is a form of racism."

Spiritual Genocide

The heads of most of the states which took the anti-Zionist line hardly knew what "Zionism" meant; in this respect, alas, they were at one with the representatives of other nations and generations which have lately emerged on the stage of history. Ignorance is sometimes grotesque. Haitian exiles have demonstrated against the "Zionism" of Papa Doc, and rebels in the Chad have declared their intention of eliminating the "Zionist clique" holding power in N'djamena. In Iran, the Ayatollah Khomeini sees "Zionists" under every bed; it is of course they who organized the assault on the Great Mosque in Mecca (November 1979). The head of state of Iraq may or may not have been amused at being described by the Ayatollah (May 1980) as "a notorious agent of imperialism and Zionism."

The others—more sophisticated—know very well what Zionism means. It is with malice aforethought that they revive the pestilential memories of a past age.

Homicide and, even more so, genocide are not political matters, but crimes.

---

[1] Article in the *Journal de Genève*, Geneva, 23 February 1977.

Some imagine they can evade responsibility by hiding behind the administrative aspects of a criminal case. I remember German clerks-of-the court in occupied France, quite indifferent to the matters at stake and anxious only to get into town before the curfew.

When "spiritual" genocide is thought easier than the physical kind, a false bureaucratic serenity is just as guilty an attitude. The government of France, an accomplice in the decision taken by the UNESCO General Conference in November 1974 to exclude Israel from the UNESCO European Region, felt obliged to explain its abstention in the vote by saying that it had in similar fashion opposed the inclusion of the United States in the European Region (unsuccessfully, as it happened). Camouflage or genuine bad faith? In any case, the explanation was entirely inadequate, since everybody knew that the United States, if excluded from the European Region, would have been included in the American one (and in any event ran no risk of "moral annihilation,"[2] unlike Israel). Incidentally, the U.S.S.R. managed to get itself included in two regions, the European and the Asian. By what right are the Russians in Asia except as a result of Czarist colonization? Perhaps the enemies of Israel (such as are in good faith) would care to face this question.

Pouring oil on troubled waters, the UNESCO secretariat, an executive body which cannot be held responsible for majority decisions taken by government delegations, then issued a press release observing that "Israel has not been excluded from UNESCO" and "could take part, as an observer, in UNESCO regional conferences, European or other, as has been the case in the past." To take another example going back to the occupation of France during the Second World War, we might recall that Parisian Jews not yet deported but forced to wear the yellow Star of David and hence earmarked for deportation were entitled to travel only in the rearmost car of subway trains. It could with equal justice have been claimed that "the Jews have not been excluded from public transport and can, by entering the rearmost car, use the Paris public transport system as before." Our enemies, never at a loss for a sophistry, invariably state that at the following session of the UNESCO General Conference, in October–November 1976, Israel was in fact included in the European Region, the automatic majority on that occasion having yielded to "American financial blackmail." So what? Without the financial and

---

[2]From a protest published by French intellectuals, among whom was the Jewish intellectual P. Vidal-Naquet, who can hardly be suspected of Zionist sympathies.

military power of the United States, the Second World War would almost certainly not have ended in the defeat of Germany. Should the risk of losing the war have been taken? It is a grave matter (but our sophists fail to understand that it is grave *for them*) that "financial blackmail" has to be resorted to (as when Hitler was to be overthrown) to save lives and human freedoms. Incidentally, the enemies of the Jewish nation, once convinced that the Americans were going to pay their entirely disproportionate contribution to the United Nations system, lost no time in setting the well-oiled machinery of anti-Zionism in motion again, once more condemning Israel *before* despatching any fact-finding body to ascertain how matters stood.

When bad faith reaches these scandalous proportions, it is absurd to react as though the rule of law still obtained, and to plead a cause. At the beginning of the century, the Dreyfus affair dishonoured half of France; the only possible reaction was to defend Dreyfus, even if he had been guilty. Whether he was guilty or not paled into insignificance against the ignoble plot of which he was the victim, the aim of which was to insinuate that no Jew could be an officer in the French Army, or if he was, then only as the agent of some foreign power.

Similarly, Israel is under no obligation to justify its policies as long as its right to existence is not fully recognized—as long as it is denied the right to have policies of its own.

But the adversary is astute enough, and his propaganda sufficiently powerful, to ensure that it is the Israelis who are expected to bear the burden of proof, and to prove that they are entitled to set up a sovereign state with all the attributes of sovereignty, including those which can be condemned only in the name of a code of ethics which nation states have hardly ever observed. These rights seem so natural to Israelis that, faced with incomprehension and hostility, they tend to retreat into an attitude combining lucidity with exasperation—an attitude I understand even if I think it may be tactically unfortunate.

Some people imagine, or try to spread the belief, that "Zionist propaganda" is backed by formidable resources and exercises enormous influence, it being assumed that only by underhand means can Zionists influence opinion. This, at any rate, is the line pursued by anti-Zionist propaganda, the resources of which are today almost limitless. Thus, His Excellency Abdallah Fadel, Algerian Minister for Youth and Sport, credits Zionism with "information media of a power unprecedented in history." He goes on to say, and it is worthwhile quoting him in full:

While the name of Goebbels remains in the memory of man as the very symbol of successful propaganda, the irony of history has it that his victims, or rather those who claim to have been his victims on the strength of other people's corpses, should have become his spiritual heirs. They have spun a remarkable spider's web around the world and their capital, Tel Aviv, is a formidable centre for the transmission of propaganda, relayed by the mass media and diplomacy of Imperialism; by such means they have had considerable success in hoodwinking world public opinion.[3]

History is here distorted in a way reminiscent of the *Protocols of the Elders of Zion* (note the imagery of the spider's web) and is redolent of the fanaticism of those who this time hope to bring about a real Final Solution. Hitherto, attempts to accomplish this latter have been foiled by Israeli resistance, so that for the time being recourse must be had to more circuitous methods. Israel's enemies feel that moral denigration is less risky than armed assault. In politics, there is a sense in which the more innocent the victim, the more vulnerable he is, because unprepared, whereas his enemies can furbish their arms and choose their time and place.

Adolf Hitler showed the way; the millions he caused to be arrested, despoiled, interned, deported, gassed or incinerated were all, of course, guilty of jeopardizing the peace and health of the community. We shall see below that the example has not passed unnoticed.

A War on Three Levels

Hitlerian oppression did not take on its final form overnight. Intermediate steps were required (minor persecution and harassment, humiliation, arrests, etc.), the overall strategy emerging only gradually (registration, wearing of the Star of David or an armband, assembly in ghettoes and camps, deportation). The final aim—extermination—was never clearly revealed.

An ideological assault on the same three levels has been launched against Israel (designed to run parallel with military pressure, economic action, and so on), notably in the international organizations.

Firstly, the enemies of Israel produce, or rather traduce, factual arguments.

[3]UNESCO General Conference, Nineteenth Session, Nairobi, Kenya, 1976, Vr/19 Prov.

Sometimes the facts are invented; they are always used tendentiously. Here are some of the more significant examples of this form of attack, which is still being pressed home.

At the UNESCO General Conference (held once every two years), Israel has since November 1974 been condemned for profanation of Christian and Moslem holy places in Jerusalem by reason of the archaeological excavations it has undertaken; the result is always a resolution calling on it to desist forthwith. For the sponsors of these resolutions, Jewish holy places do not exist. Jordan is one of the sponsors and cannot, therefore, be accused of desecrating the nonexistent between 1948 and 1967.

In February 1975, Israel was condemned by the United Nations Human Rights Commission for the arrest of Monsignor Hilarion Capucci; the arrest had been a grave affront to this prelate's cloth and the religion he represented. His immediate release was demanded. The authors of the relevant resolution depict him, at one and the same time, as innocent of the charge of transporting lethal weapons and as a major figure in the Arab resistance movement.

In May 1975, Israel was condemned at the World Health Assembly (the supreme organ of the World Health Organization) for refusing entry to a fact-finding committee the members of which had been appointed by countries notoriously hostile. By its refusal Israel had gravely jeopardized health conditions among the Palestinian Arabs (it had already been decided that those conditions were bad, the responsibility being attributed solely to Israel). Israel was called upon to admit the committee without delay. This condemnation completely ignored a statement by the head of the Israeli delegation to the effect that Israel was ready to grant every facility to a committee of that kind provided its members were nationals of countries maintaining diplomatic relations with Israel.

In March 1977, at the United Nations Conference on Water Resources, Israel was accused of making an "illegitimate use of water resources in Palestine." Note that this conference was convened in Mar del Plata, Argentina, a country in which terrorism is widespread and "anti-Semitism is on the increase; synagogues are machine-gunned and the works of Goebbels and Rosenberg are published."[4] Nevertheless, the United Nations regularly convenes major conferences there. Water supplies are of course a matter of vital and intimate concern to everybody, and of all countries Israel probably had most to teach as regards action against

[4]*Le Monde*, Paris, 27–28 March 1977.

drought. However, when the Israeli delegate asked for the floor, the Arab delegates and their satellites left the hall.

It comes as something of a surprise that the World Meteorological Conference held in Geneva in April and May 1979 passed no resolution condemning Israel for the deplorable weather obtaining at that time. After all, at the International Women's Conferences organized by the United Nations and held in Mexico City (1975) and Copenhagen (1980), resolutions were adopted condemning Zionism as one of the most serious obstacles to the emancipation of women. At those conferences, of course, nobody mentioned the womenfolk of the Moslem world—veiled, cloistered, repudiated (and liable to be stoned or beheaded if guilty of adultery or of attempting to reject the sexual restraints imposed on them). Attempts to raise the question of the barbaric sexual mutilation of girls practised in a number of African and Arab countries were nipped in the bud.

Secondly, Israel is subjected to sweeping general attacks. It is accused of, and condemned for, abominable crimes. It matters little whether the facts of the case are real or imaginary; the hope is that isolated, subjected to multiple, convergent assaults, abandoned by its former friends, the country will in time collapse of its own accord. Israeli's enemies proceed by stages; the country's exclusion from the international community will be specifically demanded only later.

Thirdly, and most important, there is a campaign to challenge the very existence of Israel. The masses, who see this country only through a veil of hostile propaganda, must be induced to believe that the Jewish homeland is incompatible with anything good, valuable, or true. They must be led to believe that if Israel impudently continues to exist, it is nevertheless essentially evil, negative, and degrading, and richly deserves destruction.

In the examples given above, the purpose goes far beyond the ostensible gravity of the complaint. In UNESCO, complaints about archaeological excavations are a pretext for *denying Jews their folk-memories*; in the Human Rights Commission, in a context such that any other country would invoke the dictates of *national security*, Israel's right to *self-defence* is impugned. In no case are Jews allowed to have a *faith* of their own. In the World Health Organization, under a pretext which could not (and did not later) withstand examination by an impartial body, Israel was depicted as somehow incompatible with the idea of *health*. At the conference on water resources, Israel was accused of exploiting a *source of life* for its own selfish purposes.

Thus is built up a portrait of a people with neither roots nor history, with no right to security or self-defence; a people without belief, defiling the faith of others; a people unhealthy and propagating disease, while monopolizing resources and thereby creating drought and famine. We thus come back to the "Jew" depicted by classical anti-Semitism, a blot on mankind, responsible for every evil.

It is sometimes said that too much importance should not be attached to violent language, which is interpreted as a sign that the Arabs themselves are aware of the impending need to recognize the reality of Israel. In this view, ritual imprecation is a means of covering up a retreat.

Unfortunately, with the passage of time people forget what reality is and come to accept the myths with which they are bombarded. The enemies of Israel know this only too well. Their ritual imprecations in effect encourage massacre and justify it in advance.

To take the question of excavations in Jerusalem, it seems to me (although this may be a shocking thing to say) that it is a matter of relative indifference whether or not Israelis have imperiled a Moslem stairway or a Christian crypt by digging a tunnel five or ten feet out of true. Not because I am certain that their measurement of angle and distance is always entirely accurate, nor because I am indifferent to the remains of civilizations other than Jewish, but simply because the enemies of Israel are perfectly aware that this is not the point. It serves no purpose, therefore, to prove that these excavations not only do not threaten Christian and Moslem monuments but reveal fresh vestiges of the past. It serves no purpose because for the sponsors of the anti-Israeli resolutions and for others only too eager to be convinced, Israel is condemned in advance. Their real aim is to inculcate the idea that the rebirth of a Jewish nation in a Jewish national state is a monstrous aberration, and that the dispersal of the Jews and the denial of their national identity are normal and irreversible. Hence they feel it essential to suggest that there is no such thing as Hebrew civilization, to deny that it can have left traces of its passage, to prevent such traces from being brought to light, and to ensure that this civilization can never be reborn. This being so, whether the Jewish claim to Jerusalem is sound or not, whether some points appear incontrovertible while others are open to argument—all this is irrelevant. In any event, the Jewish case is rejected in advance, without investigation and without appeal. Winding up the debates which in 1974 excluded Israel from every "region" into which, for UNESCO purposes, the world is divided, the delegate of Lebanon peremptorily declared that "Israel is nowhere because it comes from nowhere."

Clearly, the Israeli authorities did not arrest Monsignor Capucci because of his

100   THE ANTI-ZIONIST COMPLEX

cloth or to show disrespect for Christianity. Why should they? It was, on the contrary, because of their respect for his position that they had granted him quite exorbitant privileges and they hesitated long before arresting him in the act. Similarly, Israel combats the *fedayeen*, not because they include within their ranks the odd poet or playwright, but because they are killers. In France (1944) there was a similar campaign to arouse pity for Robert Brasillach, the right-wing author and friend of Germany (shot at the Liberation), on the grounds that he was a man of letters.

Point of No Return

This point was passed at the sixtieth session of the International Labour Conference, held in Geneva in June 1975 (its decisions with respect to Israel were echoed by the United Nations that November). This conference, which meets once a year, is the supreme organ of the International Labour Organization, the only "tripartite" specialized agency of the United Nations. (In the others, delegations consist of government representatives only; in the ILO, they contain representatives of workers' trade unions and employers' associations as well, and these representatives, unless they come from a country dictatorially governed, are free to depart from the instructions given to their governmental colleagues.) Hence it is to the honour of the worker delegations of Australia, Canada, Colombia, the Federal Republic of Germany, Sweden and the United Kingdom that they tried their utmost to oppose the admission of the PLO with observer status. Not that they refused the Palestinian Arabs the right to be represented; they acted as they did for the sake of consistency, considering that all peoples, notably those denied a right of representation by the Arab League and the Organization of African Unity, should in this respect be on the same footing. In addition, they wished to foil the rejectionists in their ultimate aim, which was and remains to get the Hebrew people expelled from the international fold. Hence this handful of worker delegations tried to put a stop to illegality by proposing an amendment to the resolution calling for PLO admission; that amendment demanded that the liberation movement in question provide some assurance that it fully recognized the principles of the ILO, as enshrined in its constitution, together with the right of all member states to existence and to participation in ILO activities—nothing more. This amendment was rejected. With a hypocrisy which is a tribute to the mask of virtue affected by international diplomacy, nobody dared oppose it openly, but because of numerous abstentions, including those of the government of France and the French workers' delegation, the quorum was not reached, and the amendment fell.

Note that it was by *abstention* that a majority of governments, workers' trade unions, and employers' associations granted admission to a movement which had refused outright to abide by the constitution of the organization concerned. This collective act of self-abasement was a considerable achievement for the Arab League and the PLO. They had, in fact, achieved more than they had bargained for; the arrow aimed at Israel had wounded all those not bold enough openly to defend that country (and their own long-term interests) or to call for its destruction.

In June 1977, at its sixty-third session, the same conference (again, thanks to mass abstention) disavowed its own principal committee—the Committee on Application of Standards—on the grounds that it had considered a report duly submitted, in accordance with the rules, by the government of Israel on the position obtaining in the occupied territories. Mr. Ibrahim (Iraq): "It was not the right of the Committee to accept and examine a report submitted by an illegal authority."[5] We thus arrive at a rule to which, for the militant anti-Zionists, there can be no exception, namely: Israel can and must be attacked on every possible occasion, for it deserves attack. Self-defence is not permitted; indeed, it is impossible, for Israel does not exist. The country is therefore at one and the same time a universal scapegoat, Satan, and a void.

At the twenty-eighth session of the World Health Assembly (May 1976), the majority achieved in this respect a major triumph by *rejecting* a report on "public health in the occupied territories" submitted by three experts (an Indonesian, a Roumanian and a Senegalese) appointed by the assembly itself in the hope that it would be able to pilot their conclusions in an acceptable direction. As a show of goodwill, the government of Israel had finally agreed to admit these experts; they, allowed freedom of movement and to draw their own conclusions, submitted a report which was, on the whole, *favourable* to Israel. For the automatic majority, this was unthinkable; to behold its own ineptitude and partiality revealed for all to see would have been too grievous a humiliation. Something had to be done, and quickly. The three experts were disavowed (by their own governments into the bargain) and called upon to redraft their report "in collaboration with the Arab

[5] Record of Proceedings, 28th Sitting, 63rd Session, 20 June 1977.

States concerned and the PLO." This did not prevent them from submitting a report on similar lines to the thirty-first session in May 1978. On this occasion, however, the assembly was not to be thwarted. It condemned Israel and threatened it with expulsion from the World Health Organization.

What Makes Israel Innocent

In this fashion, the international community has become the instrument and victim of a conspiracy. It is the essence of the community which has suffered, while the essence of Israel, ostensibly the only target, has remained untouched. The enemies of that country, by pursuing their campaign to patently absurd lengths, thereby discredit themselves and make manifest the innocence of their intended victim.

They had hoped to bring about the destruction of Israel once and for all. Israel had simultaneously to be accused of crimes against history, faith, health, progress, the rights of women, water resources, and anything else one likes to think of. In a word, Israel had to be condemned for ritual murder, in accordance with the principles applied by the Inquisition and put into effect at the Soviet show-trials. In fact, the action taken by the enemies of Israel has redounded against themselves and the international organizations they hoped to protect by abstention, or to dominate, even if by so doing they were to reduce these organizations to moral bankruptcy. In reality, these unsavoury maneuvers, these cheap triumphs, represent a colossal failure, from which are exempt, in the last resort, Israel and those few faithful friends who in rallying round demonstrated their integrity while proving that they knew where their true interests lay. For they had grasped that exclusion of Israel from the community of mankind would be fatal to the very essence of a universal community.

When countries attack Israel in this way, it is not just to hide their own sins and failures, and not just because they are fearful for their oil supplies. It is because the government of Guinea, among others, uses torture as a means of holding on to power; it is because the Soviet Union uses psychiatric internment as a political tool—to take only two countries as examples of deteriorating standards—that Israel has to be accused of every crime. They have reason to have uneasy consciences and to fear the testimony of Israel as Cain feared the sight of God.

It might be thought that to introduce a metaphysical dimension into the question is to do too much honour to the kind of accusation brought against Israel. Unfortunately, things are not so straightforward, and to imagine that a phenomenon such as National Socialism, for instance, can be understood without reference to this dimension, and explained away by the Treaty of Versailles, German unemployment under the Weimar Republic, Hitler's paranoia, etc., is to fall short of the mark. Hitler began by burning books; he was bound to go on to the burning of people. He would have incinerated God if he had been able to. For him, as for his disciples today, mass homicide was a substitute for deicide.

Clearly, innocence is no intrinsic attribute of the government of Israel or of any other government. But partial guilt is just what Israel's enemies cannot admit. For they condemn the country, it government and people, lock, stock and barrel, as wicked by definition and guilty of the deliberate pursuit of evil. And in a sense the innocence of Israel derives from the very outrageousness of the charges brought against the country. The French Huguenot poet Agrippa d'Aubigné, in a splendid phrase, wrote of those who had perished in the sixteenth-century French religious wars: "They are clad in white and washed in pardon." Every Gypsy, every Jew entering the gas chambers was washed clean of sin by the overwhelming guilt of his murderers.

The Mirror Image of Distorted Thinking

The older type of anti-Semitism, based on outright racial prejudice, is unfashionable today, and the modern anti-Zionist, whether by calculation or because he is a product of his times, tends to avoid it. He has therefore invented a neo-anti-Semitism, the logical inconsistencies of which are to some extent masked by ambiguity. Briefly to recapitulate:

Aggression: Even if attacked, Israel is always the aggressor, since it is anyway entitled to nothing.

Archaeology: All peoples look to archaeology for signs of continuity with the past. But the innumerable traces of a Hebrew past in Palestine prove nothing.

Class struggle For "revolutionaries," a panacea for everything, except in Israel. Even the South Vietnamese bourgeoisie was "objectively" anti-American. But the Israeli working class is "fascist."[6]

Colonialism: An Israeli who feels at home in Israel is a colonialist. When Messrs. Arafat and Hawatmeh, while organizing the killing of Jews, declare their willingness to tolerate such Jews as will not be expelled from some future Palestinian "secular" State, they are innocent of colonialism.

Development: Economic and social development is everywhere desirable, but not in Israel.

Diplomatic relations: It is right and proper for a country to break off diplomatic relations with Israel, "tool of American imperialism," but China sees nothing wrong in reestablishing relations with the United States. Relations between the United States and some Arab countries have been reestablished, not without some back-slapping.

Fidelity to the past: A virtue, except Jewish fidelity to Jerusalem.

Historic rights: The Jews possess none anywhere; all other peoples possess them.

Holy places: These can be Moslem or Christian. They are defiled by the presence of Jews.

Honour; humiliation: To be used only after the adjective "Arab." Who ever heard of Jewish honour? Who ever heard of humiliation suffered by Jews?

Immigration: The Jews, being sovereign nowhere, are not entitled to grant asylum to their brethren. The Soviet Union is wrong, of course, in allowing "Zionists" to emigrate, even in small numbers, and the British were quite right to fire on Jewish immigrants during the Mandate.

Jus soli: Does not apply to a Jewish child born in Israel. Similarly, in France, during the German occupation, with Jewish children born of foreign parents; later, when repression became more severe, not applicable to Jewish child-

[6] *L'Humanité rouge* (Trotskyist), Paris, April 1969.

ren born of French citizens. If not deported or gassed, such children learned from the French press that they were a "canker" (term now applied to the State of Israel).

Land: "Belongs to the man who tills it" (Bertolt Brecht), except when he happens to be a Jew.

Military conquest: The basis and foundation of nearly every nation, whether or not officially recognized by treaty. But any land conquered by Jews is "usurped" and must be handed back without reservation or compensation.

Minorities: The international community loses no sleep over the fact that there are over a hundred such in the U.S.S.R. Iraq and the Islamic Republic of Iran are perfectly entitled to massacre their Kurds. The Jews, however, have no right to cease being a minority and certainly no right to constitute a majority.

Nation: Any former colony, on independence, can call itself a nation, even if it be no more than a mosaic of peoples with frontiers inherited from a colonial past, with no unity of language, history or civilization, and even if it violently suppresses any attempt by a minority (the Ibos in Biafra, for instance) to assert their independence. The Jews are not entitled to found a nation—as though a sick man should be refused the right of recovery on the grounds that sickness is his proper state.

National defense: Any state is entitled to concentrate troops on territory it claims as its own (Egypt in the Sinai in May 1967; Syria on the Golan Heights in 1973). But the news, or rather the false rumour, that Israel had reinforced its defenses on the Syrian frontier in May 1967 was a legitimate *casus belli*.

Negotiations: The United Nations Charter specifically calls for the negotiated settlement of disputes. In all cases (but not in the case of the Arab-Israel conflict), refusal to negotiate is condemned.[7]

---

[7] The Portugal of Salazar and Caetano was condemned for failure to negotiate with the representatives of its overseas territories. "At a press conference Mr. Leopold Senghor (Senegal) said: 'We have always tried to reach agreement with Portugal.' In the United Nations, Mr. Abdoulate Touré (Guinea) accused Portugal of refusing discussions." (*Le Monde*, Paris, 20 December 1969)

Presence: From Prague to the Kuriles, from Karelia to Erevan, the Russians are legitimately present. The Jews: nowhere.

Progressive: Any Arab, and especially Arab Moslem movement, is *ipso facto* "progressive"; and the French press was quite right in describing the parties involved in the Lebanese civil war as Palestinian Arab "progressives" v. Christian Arab "conservatives." No Israeli movement can claim to be "progressive"— except perhaps Matzpen (a tiny handful of Israeli anti-Zionists who, while living in Israel, will have no truck with that country and believe that a solution of Middle East problems depends on a Trotskyist revolution which only they can bring about).

Refugees: The Palestinians are the only refugees who cannot and must not be absorbed elsewhere; their fate is to be played up as the mirror image of the Wandering Jew. As regards other refugees, notably the Vietnamese, the Arab press rightly speaks of a "forced exodus of population as a result of panic spread by *agents provocateurs*."[8] The Jewish refugees from Arab countries ought to have stayed where they were, "protected" or maltreated at the whim of the government concerned.

Reprisals: The killers of Israelis have right on their side, since they represent a people expelled. The Israelis are not entitled to hit back, since an organized state cannot allow itself the liberties legitimately claimed by guerrillas. It is no use arguing that Jews, too, have been expelled by Arab countries, or that their killers are powerfully armed by organized (Arab) States.

Resistance: Those who claim to resist Israel have right on their side. The Israelis have no rights, not even that of self-defence. The Palestinian resistance movement is quite right in supporting Soviet oppression of Russian Jews.

Rich; poor: Any Arab emirate is free to accumulate in a day, thanks to royalties, what Israel collects in a year through the heaviest taxes in the world. Nevertheless, Israel is a rich country, and the emirate a poor one.

---

[8]*El Moudjahid*, Algiers, 2 April 1975.

Secular institutions: Demanded only of the Israelis in a part of the world where religion, sometimes fanatical, infuses the whole of life.

Settlement: Were the Jews there before the Arabs? Perhaps, but there is such a thing in law as prescription. Did they arrive later? Yes, and expropriated Arab land.

Socialism: For a King of Saudi Arabia or Emir of Kuwait, Israel is too socialist; for a Colonel Qaddafi of Libya or a Dr. Hawatmeh, not socialist enough. None of these persons is in a position to engage in ordinary polemics with Israel, which is the very heart and essence of what they most detest.

Solidarity: Long live Arab, African, Arab-African, Afro-Asian solidarity! Down with solidarity between Jews of the Diaspora and their brethren in Israel! Such solidarity is suspect, even dangerous, and there is dark talk of "double allegiance."

Statelessness: When peculiar to Jews, as it was for centuries, a term of reproach or contempt. Now that the Jews are no longer stateless, why do they hesitate to revert to their former status?

Sufferings: It is in exceedingly bad taste to do as the Jews do, i.e., remember and use as an argument the millions of Jews put to death or persecuted. It is permissible to speak of Babi Yar, but not to indicate that the victims were Jews. Otherwise (argument to be adopted in the last resort, used by Nasser and Darquier de Pellepoix, a French Commissioner for Jewish Affairs under the Occupation), talk of death and persecution is simply calumny.

Territories: Leonid Brezhnev thunders against Israeli expansionism from somewhere in Roumanian Bessarabia, an area annexed by the Czars, handed back by Lenin, and again annexed by Stalin.

The West: Detestable when it takes the form of Israel, but not so when personified by Lebanon. Note that for the Western anti-Semite the Jew is to be disliked because not Western enough. Note again that Western aid is bad only when extended to Israel. Soviet aid is never bad because never given to Israel.

One could continue on these lines; the reader may like to try his hand. What is important is to observe the tone employed. Our enemies rarely refer to Israel as an adversary, for an adversary can be fought and negotiated with. Israel has to be abominated; should it refuse to bow to unilateral demands, it must be "punished" (as Sadat once said, before the events of 1977). Such is not the language of political argument, nor even of the battlefield, but of the Inquisition or the reformatory. President Sadat is to be congratulated on having promoted Israel to adversary status, a dignity still refused by the rejectionist camp. As the latter sees it, the image of the Jew is to be inverted, as in classical demonology the Fallen Angel is depicted falling head downwards, because those for whom Judaism is a continual reproach feel unable to oppose it openly. Hence the Jews must be brought low by indirect means. Once they are down, the victors may rejoice in a display of magnanimity.

Anti-Zionism thus elaborates a whole system of political references (I dare not say political analysis, nor even political reflection) in which double standards and inverted terms are constant features. Should Israel be as much as mentioned, a machinery for the projection of obsessive hallucinations comes into play. The anti-Zionist thinks, or pretends to think, in black and white.

If therefore Israel is attacked as much for what it may do as for what it does, it will be just as guilty for what it does not do. After the arms embargo decreed by General de Gaulle on 6 January 1969, the French journal *Témoignage chrétien* (which we have already encountered) published a photograph showing a deserted dock in Marseilles, with crates of arms under embargo. The caption ran: "Arms against Cairo, Damascus or Amman?" As an attempt to mislead, this takes some beating. The crates in question would have reinforced Israel at a time when the Arab countries were still receiving all the arms they needed or could buy. For the editors of this paper, the thought that Jews should no longer be weaponless was, clearly, unbearable. That Jews should possess the equipment needed to strike back would be heresy indeed. On this single point—for in all else this paper was and is anti-Gaullist—the editors approved the general.

Israel is nevertheless accused of the use to which it *might* put the arms denied it. That Israel should bomb an Arab capital would be criminal, and even a rumour that it is contemplating such a thing is held against it.

During the Second World War, these were the tactics used by the press favourable to National Socialism to whip up feeling against the Jews. Not daring openly to call for their destruction, it rejoiced to see their "influence" reduced, while continuing to denounce them for their diabolical omnipotence and the abominable crimes of which they had been accused.

But what for Hitler revealed the Devil was not necessarily evil for his opponents. Certain anti-Jewish accusations made at the time, although tendentious, exaggerated or entirely false, might if true have been seen as creditable to the Jews (their cosmopolitanism," their part in stimulating "decadent" art, literature, philosophy, etc.). We find a similar phenomenon today. Who, according to the Arab press, was behind the student revolt in France (May 1968)? Why, the Zionists! Who was guilty, according to the Arab press, of fomenting the "Prague Spring"— that brief outburst of Czech spontaneity? The Zionists, of course! Such utterances throw a revealing light on the extent to which Arab governments are "progressive." For the West European Left, they are as unquestionably "progressive" as the Japanese were "Aryan" for the racial theorists of the Third Reich.

One Law for One's Friends, Another for One's Foes

While anything Israel does, may do, or does not do reveals that country's depravity, acts of commission or omission by other countries pass unchallenged, or are not condemned in the same way, or are treated with indulgence. In no case is anything done by a country other than Israel used as a pretext for questioning the country's existence. The anti-Zionists eschew comparisons. The more reason to attempt one here. The following instance (there are many others) is instructive.

On 27 July 1955, an "Israeli Constellation aircraft crashes in Bulgaria with its 58 occupants, apparently shot down by Bulgarian anti-aircraft fire." This statement was made in an article appearing the following day on the front page of *Le Monde*. The day after, we find a heading covering two columns on the back page: "Sixty-seven dead in an Israeli Constellation shot down over Bulgaria; Sofia's regrets." Thereafter, on 30 July, twenty-six lines at the foot of page 5 inform us that "Israel protests at attack on Constellation." In following issues of this paper, the matter is relegated to "News from Abroad" (brief miscellaneous notes) indicating that "Sofia offers reparations for Constellation" and then asking: "Was the El Al Constellation shot down by fighters?" The answer appeared the next day (3 August): "Two Migs said to have shot down Israeli Constellation." On 4 August, at the foot of the column, we read that "Those responsible for the attack will be punished." On 5 August, nothing. Lastly, on 6 August, in the middle of a column: "National funeral for the 58 victims of Constellation shot down in flames over Bulgaria." Then silence.

110   THE ANTI-ZIONIST COMPLEX

On 21 February 1973, a Libyan Boeing airliner was destroyed over the Sinai Desert, too late for the news to appear in *Le Monde* the following day. But the day after, there were four columns on the first page under the headline "Arab Countries Denounce 'Savage and Barbarous Crime' Committed by Israeli Air Force" and a leading article was eloquently headed "An Unpardonable Crime." A report from Cairo: "An Act Which Will Be Dearly Paid For" (two columns), and one from Jerusalem: "A Terrible Catastrophe" (one column). The whole of page 2 was devoted to "the destruction of the Libyan Boeing by Israeli fighters"; at the foot of the page, three comments, all highly unfavourable, reproduced from the Paris press: "A Very Serious Act," "Israel Dishonoured," and "Might Rather Than Right." On 24 February, a headline right across the second page: "Contradictions Between Various Versions of Israeli Attack" and "Mr. Waldheim Calls Incident Scandalous." The following day, two columns on page 1: "General Dayan, Claiming Responsibilities Divided, Calls for International Inquiry into Destruction of Libyan Boeing"; and four on page 3: "Jerusalem Admits Pilot Thought He Was Over Egypt" and "Israelis Criticize Behaviour of Their Forces." On 27 February, the first page informed us that "the pilot was fully qualified for the flight"; and right across page 2: "Jerusalem 'For Humanitarian Reasons' to Pay Compensation to Victims' Families" (four columns). The first official reaction from Tripoli was reported as follows: "A Planned and Premeditated Crime Says Minister of Information" (two columns), plus a reminder, in a box, headed "A Qualified Pilot." On 28 February, page 5, four columns, "According to French Air Attaché in Tel Aviv, Israeli Fighters Opened Fire on Airliner's Reactors"; below, across two columns: "Crowd Cries Vengeance at Victims' Funeral."

Le Monde for March 1973 (I summarize): On 1 March: "International Civil Aviation Organization Puts Boeing Affair on its Agenda." On 2 March: "ICAO Condemns Israel; Demands Immediate Inquiry" (note condemnation first, inquiry second). On the 3rd, news of what this newspaper euphemistically calls "Operation by Palestinian Commando in Khartoum" with a footnote about the Boeing affair to the effect that "Mr. Abba Eban denounces signs of intolerance in Israel." On the 6th, *Le Monde* announces the surrender of the Black September commando group in Khartoum, while informing us that the French CFTC labour movement (non-communist Left) condemns the attack on the Libyan Boeing. On 7 and 9 March, in connection with the hostages murdered ("executed") in Khartoum, the Boeing affair is recalled, and again in connection with the problem of oil.

We then have to wait until 17 April to learn, on the back page, that "Libyan Co-Pilot of Boeing Shot Down over Sinai Confirms Israeli Version." On 2 June, headed "According to the Press in Tel Aviv," a paragraph states that "an international fact-finding committee confirms the Israeli version concerning the Libyan Boeing shot down in February." On reading the article with care, we learn that this opinion was not that of the press in Tel Aviv, but the conclusions reached by the ICAO committee of inquiry.

By consulting another newspaper for the same dates, we can build up a rough picture of what happened. As regards the information provided for public consumption in the Soviet Union, we find the following headlines in *Izvestia* between 23 and 26 February 1973: "Fresh Acts of Banditry by Tel Aviv," "The Criminal Act of Tel Aviv," "Storm of Indignation after Crime by Tel Aviv," and "Reticences of Tel Aviv"[9] — all of them over articles signed by the *Izvestia* correspondent in Cairo. Between April and June, there is no mention whatsoever of the findings of the ICAO committee of inquiry.

These two affairs — the Israeli Constellation and the Libyan Boeing — were deplorable and tragic by any reckoning, and I have no wish to apportion blame among the parties concerned (nor to wash my hands of the matter by implying that all were equally to blame). I have simply taken two cases likely to arouse indignation against the guilty and pity for the innocent victims and tried to show that there is no common measure between the reactions when Israelis are the victims and when Israel is the guilty party (or presumed so). There is also one essential difference between the two incidents. Bulgaria and Israel have never been at war; why should the Bulgarians destroy an Israeli aircraft? But Libya considers itself permanently at war with Israel and has spent vast sums arming and training those who are to kill the men, women, children, and friends of that country.

When the acts of a state hostile to Israel go too evidently beyond the bounds of the acceptable, as happened when the "progressive" Syrians massacred Palestinians in Lebanon, Zionism is again in the dock. Thus, the Franco-Palestinian Medical Association in a statement dated 12 July 1976 declared: "The Assad Government . . . is today the main agent of imperialist and Zionist plots designed to encompass the destruction of the Palestinian resistance movement . . . and to

---

[9] The government of Israel is in Jerusalem. References to Tel Aviv in newspaper reports are a fairly reliable indication of what side the newspaper wishes its readers to sympathize with.

dismember the Lebanon, or to bring about its incorporation in a Greater Syria."[10] That the creation of a Greater Syria would be in the interests of Israel seems self-evident to the president of the association, who sees no absurdity in writing of the Tel el-Zaatar tragedy that this camp had surrendered to the "forces of fascism and reaction." He equally condemns the "usurper State of Israel" and the shades of the Fascist Goebbels (whose arguments in fact he borrows), writing:

> All this is hidden from the French, who are asked to admire the "Israeli miracle"—a logical consequence of the infantilism of French history books, exalting "Western civilization" (Goebbels spoke of "Aryan civilization") against the barbarity of the Arabs.[11]

Anyone who can pack so much absurdity into so few lines deserves admiration.

The Four Golden Rules

For a little light relief, let us take the following passage, which appeared in a Swiss paper in response to a Protestant clergyman who had commented, with some asperity, on the anti-Israel voting habits of African delegations in the United Nations:

> No, what you call anti-Zionism might simply be the difficult birth of a new awareness on the part of the Arabs and their Third World friends of the fact that at long last the course of their history, halted outside Poitiers in 732, has been resumed. They are now trying to make up for the centuries during which the world was dominated by Western Christianity.[12]

Such extravagance is not necessarily due to bad faith (not all newspapers are deliberately misleading, unlike *Izvestia*). There is no need to go back to the battles of 732 to explain a new kind of anti-Semitism. These assertions are a natural outgrowth of the lies with which public opinion is being bombarded. What is so striking in the accusations launched against Israel is not so much that they are monstrous (the "genocide" Israel is accused of practising, if "genocide" there be, is

[10] *Le Monde*, Paris, 14 July 1976.
[11] *Le Monde*, Paris, 22 July 1976.
[12] G. de Rougement, in *La Suisse*, Geneva, 6 August 1975.

as nothing compared to the massacre of the Armenians, which has remained unpunished, and even unacknowledged); it is not that they are absurd—Idi Amin Dada, when still in power, said and did plenty of absurd things quite apart from his judgments on Israel. Thus, Simon Malley, a notorious enemy of Israel, writes that it was "revolting to see General Idi Amin Dada, who had fought only once, as a sergeant in the British colonial army, and then against his Mau Mau brethren in Kenya, propose to send ten thousand men to Angola."[13] What is striking is the basic incompatibility supposed to exist between Israel and the rest of the world by the inveterate anti-Zionists. The following golden rules can be deduced, applicable in all circumstances:

1. Anything Israel does is to be condemned.
2. Israel is to be condemned even if it does nothing.
3. Nothing done by another country, even if indistinguishable from something done by Israel, can provide a parallel or a precedent, and if the comparison is made, then always to Israel's disadvantage.

To these three eternal verities can be added another, derived from the propaganda successes attributable to application of the first three:

4. Since Israel is inevitably in the dock, any action, no matter how monstrous, can be taken against it with impunity. This was the PLO attitude at the fourth session of the Diplomatic Conference on Humanitarian Law (Geneva, April 1977), at which the PLO representative explained that "this principle applied not only to the position obtaining in the territories occupied in 1967, but throughout Palestine, occupied in 1948; to combat racial oppression in every case gave entitlement to prisoner of war status."[14] In plain language this means: "I am entitled to kill the Cohen family, including infants in the cradle, and you are under an obligation to treat me as a prisoner of war."

Let us, however, be careful to invert the terms; at the Olympic Games in Munich, the killers were victims and the victims, killers. Ethics, like logic, must be turned upside-down.

The policy of *apartheid* is today universally abhorred. It so happens, however, that Israel itself is a victim of it. At the Asian Games in Teheran (September 1974), certain countries, while ready to compete with Israel in events such as track,

[13]*Afrique-Asie*, Paris, 11 August 1975.
[14]*Le Monde*, Paris, 24–25 April 1977.

swimming, etc., withdrew from face-to-face encounters. The Chinese, unchallenged masters of ping-pong diplomacy, the North Koreans (fencing), and the Pakistanis (basketball) refused to play with Israelis.

Yet Zionism itself, and not only the current policies of the Israeli government, is constantly accused of being equivalent to *apartheid* simply because it represents a national emancipation movement which differs from others in being Jewish.

The fate of the Third Reich has shown that a policy of death and destruction contains the seeds of its own doom; such a policy, systematically pursued, is suicidal. The great misfortune of the Palestinians is not to be found in what the anti-Israelis claim the Palestinians have to endure. It lies in the PLO itself, an instrument of death. Conversely, the great hope of Israel lies in that hope itself.

Israel and the Fourth World

In various parts of the world, despite all efforts to quench it, there burns the flame of hope. The longer attempts at extinction continue, the more violent the resulting explosion is likely to be. The same cowardly connivance or resignation which during the Second World War smothered the voices raised in Warsaw and Treblinka today prevents the world from hearing the voice of the Crimean Tartars, expelled to Central Asia, or that of the Baltic peoples, deported or oppressed by the greatest and most inflexible of contemporary colonial powers. The Armenians, an ancient people, are beginning to remind the world of their existence. Elsewhere—in Kurdistan, Nagaland, ex-Portuguese (now Indonesian) Timor, Biafra, Tibet—the standard of revolt has been raised, and it would be wrong to be too easily convinced by official propaganda that resistance has been put down or is dying out.

The United Nations, with the approval of a majority of its members, which have an interest in seeing the matter overlooked, glosses over the fact that in many so-called decolonized Third World countries there is no more freedom than in the so-called socialist camp, and that minorities in these countries are even worse off. The potentates in power have every interest in covering up this fact and hence shout the more loudly against the real or supposed crimes of the West. They know that special indulgence is extended to both the "decolonized" and the "socialist" worlds. Yet the crimes they commit are all the graver for running counter to the "historical trends" they like to acclaim as irresistible. But while the crimes committed in the communist world are now to some extent common knowledge since Nikita Khrushchev opened the sluice-gates in 1956, nothing equivalent to the XXth Party Congress has yet taken place to reveal the skeletons in the cupboards of the Third World.

A list of peoples of the Fourth World today suffering under newly instituted tyranny would be long. One example must suffice. The island of New Guinea, north of Australia, is inhabited by a conglomerate of peoples long subject to colonial rule. In the west of the island power was wielded by the Dutch, who in 1956 handed over to the Indonesians, who had no more right to be there than the Dutch had but were in no way ready to surrender power to the natives; they were never in fact called upon to do so. The eastern part of the island was governed by the Australians. They, sensitive to international opinion as represented by the United Nations, perhaps by conviction, perhaps from considerations of self-interest, granted a far-reaching autonomy in 1973 and full independence in 1975. The government now in power in Indonesia, be it observed, has in its time massacred communists by the hundred thousand, earning (1965–1966) vehement criticism from the U.S.S.R. This state of affairs did not last; today, the Soviet Union and Indonesia display their community of interests by denouncing "crimes against humanity" committed by Israel.

But beginning in 1977, the press announces that the natives of West New Guinea, like the Moluccans or the people of Timor, are up in arms against their new masters in Djakarta. The numerous peoples of Soviet Europe and Asia, the numerous minorities in Black Africa and the Arab world and those in the subcontinent of India, will not remain forever gagged. What these peoples, ignored by those who make a living out of the "hell" endured by others, need is an effective spokesman, a Franz Fanon[15] or perhaps a Stokely Carmichael of the Fourth World (though it is to be hoped that they find one less wordy and more rigorous in analysis than those two individuals).

The oppressors, if they remain deaf and blind, are in for an unpleasant surprise, for sooner or later their victims (or the survivors) will demand a rendering of accounts, as did the survivors of Warsaw and Treblinka. Some day or other the peoples oppressed by the new imperialist mafia will force their way into the international organizations, and the hands, often bloodstained, which today applaud Arafat will not be enough to keep the intruders out.

---

[15] The late Franz Fanon was a black doctor from French Martinique who wrote (in Europe) the influential book, *The Wretched of the Earth*, Grove Press, New York, 1965.

Israel, that intruder, is closer to the victims of Soviet and Third World colonialism in that it is itself threatened by the more fanatical representatives of both. When the late Colonel Boumedienne, having declared (it is untrue, but happened to be useful for propaganda purposes and salved his conscience) that "the Jews have for centuries lived alongside Moslems in all Arab countries with no restriction on their freedom, free from oppression and adverse discrimination of any kind," and added that "Israel must follow the Arab model," he made it impossible to believe what he had just said. Furthermore, his language was exactly like that used by French colonialists about the Algerians before the latter became independent, with just that touch of condescension which the colonized find especially wounding. With this difference—that today many anti-colonialists, by an aberration which is a political scandal and will one day have to be paid for, support Arab colonialism, whether against Israel and the Jews of Syria and Iraq or against the Kabyls, Kurds, and black Sudanese.

What brings the people of Israel closer to the peoples of the Fourth World is that all of them are victims of the same fundamental imbalance which obtains throughout the United Nations organizations and in the numerous non-governmental bodies which in this respect at least follow United Nations practice. The basic reason for the imbalance lies in the exorbitant part played in all these organizations by countries belonging to the Arab League and the Organization of African Unity. These states take advantage of the power conferred by oil and numbers, of Western feebleness, and of unconditional support from the Soviet group, to arrogate to themselves, without the slightest basis in law, the right to endorse or excommunicate national liberation movements as they may see fit. The Conference of Non-Aligned States, meeting in Algiers in 1973, drew up a list of such movements,[16] which has since that time had force of law in all international meetings.

This list made no mention of the national liberation movements of the Spanish African territories. There is a simple explanation of the omission: Franco's Spain had given unconditional support to the Arabs against Israel in all the internaional organizations. On the one and only occasion when a clash seemed possible (the Moroccan "Green March" on the frontiers of the Spanish Sahara in November 1975), the affair fizzled out, to be followed by Spanish-Moroccan collusion at the

---

[16]*Le Monde*, 8 September 1973.

expense of the Saharan peoples. From that time (though there were signs, in 1980, that the position may be changing as a result of tensions among the Arab North African countries) no representatives of these Saharan peoples, any more than representatives of the Ibos or Kurds, have enjoyed the support of these powerful backers, since their presence, even as observers, at a meeting of the "non-aligned" would be opposed either by the Arab League or by the OAU. To avoid any possible clash, these two bodies close their eyes to the struggles for national emancipation waged by the Eritreans and Somalis in the same way as they remain blind (so as not to offend the Kremlin) to the lot of the Central Asian peoples colonized by Russia. The United Nations simply accepted the Arab-African list of eligible movements, and since the Portuguese colonies gained their independence, the list has been limited to movements existing in Southern Africa, plus of course the PLO.

Such discrimination, which is of more than theoretical importance, may have grave consequences in the field of "humanitarian law" (treatment of the wounded, prisoners and civilians) during internal strife. Thus, the Diplomatic Conference on Humanitarian Law (Geneva, 1974–1977), organized by the International Committee of the Red Cross, adopted without discussion the United Nations criteria of what constitutes a national liberation movement. Hence it is not just at the expense of the Israelis that the PLO, as we have seen, has been granted priority over other movements, for such priority is prejudicial to all such movements as do not happen to enjoy Arab-African "recognition." By virtue of what criteria should a Palestinian prisoner or casualty enjoy medical care and legal protection refused to a Naga, a Kurd, or a Timorese? This is not in any way to question the immense value of the work done by the International Red Cross, but rather to impugn the maneuvers which would pervert the principles of humanity and equity whereby Red Cross representatives in the field are guided.

These privileges are over and above the various other advantages which the United Nations in the name of anti-Zionism has extended to the people the PLO claims to represent. A summary of the work of the General Assembly (32nd session), published by the United Nations Information Service in New York on 21 December 1977, is eloquent in this respect. It informs us (listing the bodies set up at the expense of member states to carry on the struggle against Israel) that "the Assembly reaffirmed its support for the plan drawn up by the Committee on the Exercise of the Inalienable Rights of the Palestinian People" (which plan invited "the Security Council to establish a calendar for the full evacuation by Israeli forces of the areas occupied in 1967"), adopted a resolution concerning the creation of a Special Unit for Palestinian Rights, and requested the Committee on Israeli Practices in the Occupied Territories to continue its work. So that the reader may be in no doubt at all as to what the Assembly felt about such "practices," we are told that it "condemned" them. There is of course no United Nations plan, drawn up by a Committee on the Exercise of the Inalienable Rights of the Czechoslovak People, for the full evacuation of Czechoslovakia by the Soviet forces which have been there since 1968. Nor, equally naturally, is there a word of condemnation for Indonesian practices in the occupied territories of the Moluccas, Timor, and West New Guinea.

Clearly, we cannot demand of the regional bodies set up by the Third World countries that they adhere more strictly to the United Nations line than the United Nations itself. Nevertheless, it is astonishing that at the eleventh Islamic Conference of Foreign Ministers (Islamabad, May 1980) the Afghan Liberation Front should have been refused admittance, even though sponsored by the Islamic Republic of Iran, and even as an observer only. From what quarter came the opposition which carried conviction with the other participants? From the PLO. This would seem to prove, if proof were needed, that these Islamic statesmen know neither what they want nor where they are going, whereas the PLO knows perfectly well what it wants, which is to be considered as the only "liberation movement" in that part of the world. The Afghan resistance movement is the victim of its so-called friends, so blinded with anti-Zionist prejudice that they neglect their own true interests, giving greater importance to anti-Zionism than to the survival of their fellow-Moslems.

No, Israel is not alone, provided its public relations specialists (not hitherto very effective) are far-sighted enough to establish the necessary ties with the forces of tomorrow. Obviously, other factors will be important as well. All the more reason to ensure that the enemy is not gratuitously offered extra weapons.

Contrary to so many hopes, there has over the last few years been a rapid decline in the standards upheld by the international organizations. Reactions in Israel and elsewhere have been slow and inadequate, perhaps because the spectacle offered has been so grotesque. Let us not forget, however, that the masquerade was originally a means of conjuring the Black Death. It was as spectacular as it was ineffective. While a mask can hide a canker, it cannot stop its spread.

An Erosion of Standards

This international masquerade, if we look closely, marks a definite decline into earlier, barbarous standards. Playing up the problems of Israel helps to distract attention from the excesses of savage dictatorial régimes. One result, noticeable everywhere, is a blunting of people's critical sense—a feature noticeable under fascism but also observable in many of those who like to think of themselves as of the "Left" (the French socialist Marcel Déat became a National Socialist under the German occupation). Today, men's ability to think clearly and independently has suffered a kind of trauma, as a result of which anti-Zionist propaganda-induced obsessions colour the public approach to entirely different problems. As regards the Third World, for instance, thoughts and feelings are mobilized on behalf of new imperialisms (those of China, Nigeria, and Iraq, among others), whereas logically it is the victims (the Tibetans, Ibos and Kurds) who should enjoy the sympathy. Throughout the world, there are now many who, themselves traumatized, are convinced that the abnormality lies in others. Among the Soviet psychiatrists acting in the Kremlin's interests by securing the arbitrary internment of dissidents, there are almost certainly some who are sincerely convinced that anybody refusing to toe the official line must be mentally abnormal.

The international spectacle would be comic if not fraught with consequences. The Belgrade Conference on Security and Cooperation in Europe broke up on 7 March 1978 after weeks of hesitation about its final communiqué, the democracies having finally bowed to the Soviet veto on any mention of human rights. It is less well-known that at about the same time (6– 24 February) there was meeting in Geneva a Special Ad Hoc Committee on the Drafting of an International Convention against the Taking of Hostages, under the auspices of the United Nations. This convention will never emerge, or if it does, will never be ratified, or if ratified, will never be applied by the countries which are accomplices in the taking of hostages, train the hostage-takers in special camps before the event, and grant them asylum afterwards. And it is hardly likely to be ratified by the governments which themselves take hostages or defend the practice of hostage-taking by their own citizens, as has been the case with the Islamic Republic of Iran. Be that as it may, the meeting led to very little, since Arab countries opposed inclusion of the following two sentences in the committee's report:

Even the proponents of the rights of national liberation movements repeatedly asserted that they were in no way suggesting to grant to these movements an open licence for the taking of hostages. Their only concern was that in the proposed Convention a distinction was to be drawn between genuine activities of national liberation movements and acts of terrorist groups which had nothing in common with them.

Under pressure from the representatives of Algeria and Libya, the committee decided, on a Canadian proposal, to amend the above to read: "In this respect, it was generally agreed that no one should be granted an open licence for taking hostages." No open licence perhaps, but also, be it observed, no categorical prohibition either. In silence, the international community prefers to look the other way.

In June 1980, during the sixty-sixth session of the International Labour Conference in Geneva, the government delegate of the United States went to the rostrum to defend his country against a bitter attack launched by the Syrian delegate, who had criticized the United States for its abstention in a Security Council vote on a text condemning bomb attacks on three Palestinian mayors. The United States representative explained that his country had abstained because the resolution in question made no mention of acts of terrorism committed against Israelis. The Arab delegates in the hall thereupon began to bang their desks, presumably demonstrating support for assassination, providing the victims were nationals of Israel. Such apology for murder is unprecedented in the history of the international organizations.

The countries which are accomplices in the attacks launched on Israel or are too shy to speak out in its defence share responsibility for the decline in international standards. While the Ad Hoc Committee was sitting, the thirty-fourth session of the United Nations Human Rights Commission was also in progress. A few figures will show that the systematic condemnation of Israel is merely one aspect of an overall distortion of values. Press release HR/607, issued on 10 March 1978 by the European Office of the United Nations in Geneva, is headed "Run-Up of Session" and purports to give a bird's-eye-view of the commission's three-week meeting. The amount of space devoted to each country or problem discussed is a pretty accurate reflection of how long the respective debates lasted and of the importance the commission attached to them.

This press release runs to just over twenty pages, of which we can neglect two pages of introduction and another three dealing with administrative matters, leaving fifteen. Of these, ten and a half are devoted to particular countries and only four and a half to an impressive array of general questions, such as economic, social, and cultural rights, the rights of children, discrimination based on religion, a draft convention against torture, migrant labour, etc. The space devoted to individual countries is revealing too. Three pages "condemn" South Africa, another three Israel (or rather the "Occupied Arab Territories, including Palestine"). Chile, where the situation is merely "deplored," has to be content with two. Cyprus and Cambodia have to share a single page. As regards the former, far from "condemning" or "deploring" or even alluding to the occupation of almost half the island by Turkish forces, the commission urges "the two Cypriot communities to seek a peaceful, just and lasting settlement." There is nothing about any settlement of the Israeli-Arab dispute, nor indeed is there any reference to the existence of two communities. As regards the slaughter in Democratic Kampuchea, the commission politely "requests" the government of that country to supply its comments; these were received by the United Nations some months later in the form of gross insults. The same government, having later been expelled from Phnom Penh by the Vietnamese, then sought with honeyed words to keep its seat in the United Nations (so far with success). One single page is quite enough for "violations of human rights in any part of the world"—i.e., in countries other than those mentioned above. Eight countries (Bolivia, Ethiopia, Equatorial Guinea, Indonesia, Korea, Malawi, Paraguay, and Uruguay) are mentioned without comment; we know nothing about them since the commission's debates were private and we are told that any action envisaged will have to remain confidential. Less than half a page is left for the immense problems of the rights of minorities, in favour of which (but they are not specified), two "draft procedural resolutions" were adopted.

Nowhere in the document is there any reference to Argentina or Tunisia (the Arab world in general is strictly taboo), nor is there any mention of the Soviet Union and the territories and countries it has occupied. There is not a word about the Iran of the Pahlavi dynasty, whose delegations had approved or sponsored all the anti-Israeli resolutions. (In 1980, this did not prevent the Islamic Republic of Iran from attacking the deposed Shah's "pro-Zionist" stance.) The Shah's breaches of human rights were denounced in the United Nations only after his fall, by the same countries which at Persepolis and elsewhere had fallen over themselves to flatter the "tyrant" and his sister Ashraf, who at one time had taken the chair at international meetings concerned, of all things, with the protection of human rights.

Another change deserves notice. Following the invasion of Afghanistan by Russian armies on 27 December 1979, the automatic majority within the United Nations has shown signs of fission, both in the Security Council and in the Human Rights Commission. Since then, the Soviet group has been challenged by the Moslem countries, supported by a majority of Third World States, Algeria and Syria remaining faithful to the U.S.S.R.

The fact that these last two countries support Russian imperialism against their Moslem brethren in Afghanistan clearly shows how little sympathy they really have for other "brethren" in Palestine, whom they champion (when they are not massacring them, as the Syrians have done in the Lebanon) only as instruments for the destruction of Israel. On the day (14 January 1980) when the Soviet Union was condemned in the United Nations General Assembly by a massive majority of 104 votes to 18, all that the PLO representative had to say was to denounce the "unilateral action taken by the United States against the Soviet Union" and the "invasion of the Indian Ocean by United States warships." Even the representative of Kuwait, one of the co-sponsors of the anti-Soviet resolution, was to declare (1 March 1980) in the Security Council that "what worries us in this part of the world is less the clatter of Soviet tanks than the instability caused by the policy of Israel."

Be it observed that the breach between the socialist and Moslem groups was brought about by a specific case of armed intervention and may be closed again at any time in the light of events. It in no way affects the stubborn campaign against Israel, the violence of which is steadily mounting to bring about the explosion both blocs desire.

Despite these reservations, it remains gratifying that at long last the world's greatest colonial power has been denounced and condemned by a majority of the states represented in the United Nations system. Nevertheless, on 14 February 1980, the United Nations Human Rights Commission, meeting in Geneva, was to adopt two resolutions, one of which urged all member states to display solidarity with the peoples of Afghanistan "in their just struggle to preserve their faith, national independence and territorial integrity," while the other declared that "the Camp David accords and other agreements have no validity." Both these resolutions appear under the same heading: "Right of Peoples to Self-Determination." Thus the United Nations manages to be against war and against peace at the same time.

This same body, at its thirty-seventh session (February– March 1981), meeting in an atmosphere charged with "murderous hatred" (to borrow language used by the representative of the United States, the one small voice of reason and decency to be raised, almost all the other Western delegations demonstrating a mixture of cowardice and indifference), adopted two resolutions directed against Israel. Although it may be tiresome to add to the list of major aberrations of which the Commission has in its time been guilty, the following quotations may be of interest to the historian when the time comes (as it will) to describe this peculiarly shabby period in the decline of the international organizations.

The Commission reiterates its statement on Camp David and "strongly condemns all partial agreements and separate treaties." Fine words, these, from the United Nations, the members of which, according to its Charter, "are determined to save succeeding generations from the scourge of war ... . to practice tolerance and live together in peace as good neighbours, to unite our strength to maintain international peace and security."

The other resolution "declares that Israel's grave breaches of the Geneva Convention . . . are war crimes and an affront to humanity." Observe that the countries which presume to act as prosecutor, judge and executive agent at one and the same time, and would be glad to give effect to a sentence passed by a political body masquerading as a court, include Argentina, Byelorussia, Cuba, Iraq, Libya, Morocco, Syria, Vietnam, and the U.S.S.R.

Some Western delegations (including that of France) thought to lessen the impact of this text by proposing that the original's "crimes against humanity" be changed to "an affront to humanity." If this shows good intentions (although personally I would rather be accused of crime than be termed an "affront"), the decline in international standards nevertheless remains painfully evident.

As to the implicit denial of Israel's right to exist to be found in the very wording of this particular item on the agenda of the Commission ("Question of the Violation of Human Rights in the Occupied Arab Territories, including Palestine"), it becomes quite explicit in the resolution, which "reiterates the alarm deeply expressed . . . that Israel's policy in the occupied territories is based on the so-called 'Homeland' doctrine." Perhaps one day the United Nations, under an agenda item worded "Question of the Violation of Human Rights in the Occupied Territory of Brittany, including Gaul," will condemn France for "basing its policies on the so-called doctrine of the 'Republic One and Indivisible.' "

The Ups and Downs of Resistance

I do not know whether the barbarians in power sleep soundly at night. They must at least be aware that they are liable to be overthrown at any time. For the moment, at any rate, their consciences may be clear, because for once in history they enjoy the blessing, open or implicit, of the international institutions set up to prevent and combat non-civilized behaviour.

This tendency to give institutional status to a profoundly antisocial principle, the sole (and declared) aim being to support the interests of a majority (assumed just by definition) may conceivably be counterproductive. Certainly, in the early stages, democratic convictions put up an extraordinarily feeble resistance to repeated assaults. The shortcomings of the contemporary West—submissiveness, lack of imagination, a guilt complex—have been all too apparent. Repeated failures in so many fields (decolonization, peace, disarmament, repression of fascism in its modern forms, the faltering campaign against hunger, the problem of relations with the Third World) have thrown the West into disarray. It faces a dilemma: either to lower itself to the standards of those who are attacking it, or to lose the battle.

The Second World War showed that the will to resist is not born at once, but is rather the fruit of bitter experience. Thus, with assistance from vitriolic anti-Zionist propaganda, the first half of the 1970s was marked by a series of episodes in which hostages were taken with complete impunity. The governments of certain Western countries fell over themselves to grant the hostage-takers' every demand and to pay colossal ransoms later used for further outrages at Europe's expense. And it is undoubtedly true that at least initially PLO hostage-taking brought enormous publicity for that movement in the world's press and hastened the day when it would secure the international recognition it coveted.

The perversion of ideology and language frequently went hand-in-hand with a perversion of another kind, of which people are rarely conscious, namely, a kind of sadomasochism, such as evidenced by the incredible affection sometimes felt by the masses for their tyrants (Russian crowds shed tears at the news of Stalin's death) and in the extraordinary complicity (barely credible to those who have not witnessed it) which grows up between victims and executioners.[17] The more

---

[17] See "The Victors" in J. P. Sartre, *Three Plays*, Knopf, New York, 1949.

odious the crime, the greater the shock. But what kind of shock? To begin with, there is indignation, gradually yielding to fascination, about which, as with drink or drugs, people are on the defensive. As the fascination grows, sympathy with the victims dwindles. During the affair at Orly Airport in Paris in January 1975, the *fedayeen* wounded eight people and to make good their escape locked their victims, including a child and a pregnant woman, in the airport lavatories for the night. During the following few days, there was much talk in the French press about the *fedayeen*, rather less about the hostages, and none at all about the wounded. However shocking this may appear, there is no doubt that for a part of public opinion at least, such events provide a spectacle of an ambiguous kind, like so many public entertainments: human or simulated sacrifices, firework displays playing on some obscure urge to arson, stock-car racing, heavyweight boxing, and the like. When hostages were taken at the Saudi Arabian Embassy in Paris (September 1973), a crowd spent the night in the street outside and grew restive when nothing happened; it calmed down thanks to a spontaneous strip-tease act. Clearly, the courage of the Kurds, who as a matter of principle have always refused to follow the Palestinian example (although they are a great deal worse off than the Palestinians), offers less in the way of popular entertainment than do hijacking, strip-tease, or hostage-taking.

The disillusioned or the prejudiced may object that a similar explanation could be offered for at least part of the public reaction to the Entebbe rescue operation by Israeli forces which saved the lives of a hundred or so Jewish hostages held by a German-Palestinian commando group with the open complicity of the despot Idi Amin Dada. Would it not be true to say that while the masses were ready to applaud an audacious and successful operation, they readily forgot the victims, whether Ugandan or Jewish, who paid for this success with their lives?

In fact it is not all that important to unravel the motives of those who for whatever reason are on the side of the angels, for even the most generous manifestation of sympathy can usually be shown to contain some small proportion of self-interest or calculation. From the point of view of political analysis, what is of interest is the psychology of the enemies of life and the fascination they can exert. We therefore miss the point if we reduce the admiration aroused by the Entebbe rescue operation to sadomasochism. The essential thing is that the operation was launched to save innocent lives, whereas aerial piracy and the taking of hostages are designed to humiliate, inflict suffering, kill—and if possible secure the release of similar killers. The reticent and the disapproving too readily forget that the Jewish hostages at Entebbe were threatened with the direst of fates as part of a strategy of blackmail and murder designed to lead up to the destruction of Israel as a nation. The Entebbe raid was not a premeditated act of war nor part of some vendetta. An act of legitimate defence, it represented for Israel a chance to wipe out the memories of Lod, Munich, Maalot, and many other crimes. It was an assurance for the Jewish people that there would be no fresh Auschwitz. For the world at large, it was an eye-opener.

It was an eye-opener in the sense that from this point on the democracies began, however dimly and sluggishly, to understand that surrender may be easier in the short run, but gravely compromises the future; that resistance may entail fearful short-term risks, but is the only possible course if the evil is to be eradicated. As bloodshed continues in various parts of the world, as people learn that German and Japanese killers have been trained in the same camp as the *fedayeen*, the chorus of praise hitherto lavished on the latter becomes a little less unanimous. Indeed, certain voices have been raised in Cairo to express frank hostility; especially was this the case after the massacre at Larnaca, Cyprus, in February 1978, which proved that the PLO was perfectly capable of treating Egyptians as though they were vulgar Zionists. That massacre, like the one perpetrated a month later on the Tel Aviv–Haifa road, plus various subsequent feats, gained no sympathy for the PLO, rather the contrary. None of its initiatives, even the attempts to use Israeli reprisals to win public sympathy, are any longer quite sufficient to arouse that active solidarity which the movement lacks (despite a good deal of applause from the sidelines) but which it requires if it is to put its plans for the destruction of Israel into effect. If these were the aims of the PLO, the target has been missed.

But Israel, too, may be said to have missed a target.

Preoccupied as it is with defence in the military sense, Israel sometimes appears too little concerned with defence in spheres where it is as legitimate and in the long run hardly less important. I do not wish to give the impression, which I often have when reading the writings of others, that I am criticizing Israel at a time when, perhaps more than ever before, it needs support and assistance. On the contrary, it is my belief that those outside Israel who possess special experience of international relations are justified in commenting from the sidelines. For it is here especially that PLO successes have been most numerous, and it is here that neither Israeli diplomacy nor the institutions which in the Diaspora are expected to defend Zionism and Jewish ideals seem equipped to parry the *ontological* onslaughts to which Israel is subjected. They tend to be altogether too defensive. All too ready to be lured into minefields specially prepared for them, they give battle on ground not of their own choosing, whereas the enemy launches his assaults against the very heart and vitals of the Jew, the Jewish people and the Jewish nation.

UNESCO, again, provides an instructive example. We have seen that in 1974 Israel was condemned for archaeological excavations in Jerusalem and was refused inclusion in any of the regional groupings among which this organization apportions its funds and activities.

Incidentally, Israel is a member of none of the three geopolitical groups which have emerged in other major organizations of the United Nations system, such as UNCTAD (United Nations Conference on Trade and Development), perhaps because its representatives have never made any effort to join. Rightly or wrongly (but in any event contrary to the strategy pursued in UNESCO) Israel belongs neither to the Third World group (to which it would doubtless be refused admission) nor to the group of the advanced industrial countries (which it does not want to join for fear that it might thereby find itself ranged against the Third World). Obviously, it could not possibly join the group made up of the East European countries. One other country is in the same position—China—but with a major difference. In every important debate, the chairman asks for the views of the three groups and then for those of China. Israel's delegation is ignored.

In 1976, after a lengthy procedural battle, this non-country was finally included at its own request in the European group of UNESCO, but was again condemned (and has since been further condemned by the 1980 UNESCO General Conference in Belgrade). The attack here was aimed at the very vitals of the nation. Yet Israeli delegations have never mounted a counterattack in defence of Israel's basic right to its own national history. They try by maneuver to mitigate the terms of the verdict passed (attempting, for instance, to get "condemns" replaced by "deplores"), as though a man who by dodging escapes the spittle directed at him somehow renders the insult less offensive. True, Israel did finally achieve inclusion in the European group, thanks very largely to the heroic silence maintained by its delegation in face of a barrage of accusations, taunts and insults. It was a Pyrrhic victory, for if there is any part of the world to which Israel naturally belongs, it is the Middle East. Such tactics make things too easy for the country's enemies. Later in 1976, when the UNESCO budget for the following few years was being discussed, the Arab countries secured the lion's share of the Middle East credits. The Iranian and Turkish delegations having protested, some satisfaction was given to Persian and Turkish cultures. But the Israeli delegation, clinging desperately to its folding seats somewhere in the European group, remained faithful to its policy of silence. Thus it is that Hebrew culture, the Yiddish variant of which was eliminated from Central and Eastern Europe by the joint effects of the Final Solution and Marxist cultural assimilationism, no longer exists, as far as UNESCO is concerned, in the very country which gave it birth, has remained its focal point, and has witnessed its resurrection.

The Israeli War of Independence in 1948 was a model revolution, the first successful redemption of an alienated people, and one of the very few revolutions not to abandon democratic processes and devour its own children. One factor in this was the messianic fervour which has never, throughout the centuries, entirely deserted the Jews. It is sad that the responsible authorities in the young State of Israel, as is the way with so many bureaucracies, should remain blind to the profit to be derived from this creative ferment in the ideological struggle. In this struggle, Israel seems all too often content to play a passive part. We shall now have to inquire whether there may not be a deeper reason for this passivity; whether or not the fact that Jewish thought has traditionally been bewildered by and unable to account for or come to terms with the persistence of Evil[18] may not have something to do with it. Some of the clumsiness or weakness in defence certainly derives from this, the more so in that the Jewish mind considers that Evil is irreversible and not to be made good once accomplished.

The question remains open. The last chapter in this book is an attempt to show the originality of Jewish messianism in face of the dominant trends in contemporary thought. If it does not provide a full answer, it will, I hope, stimulate reflection.

---

[18] See the article on "Good and Evil" in the *Encyclopaedia Judaica*.

VI
Judaism and Edenisms

We shall come to comprehend little of these problems unless we understand one essential point, namely, that the quality or state of being Jewish exists in its own right, independent of the non-Jewish environment, although inevitably there is some intermixture and confusion between Jew and Gentile, and individual Jews may secede or be assimilated. This state or quality (I abstain from any judgment of value), although difficult to discern in the kaleidoscope of existence and however deeply consciousness of it may be repressed individually or collectively, is liable at any time to reemerge in its pristine form. A man may be barely conscious or even totally unaware of his Jewishness, but the society in which he lives will never forget and is liable in certain circumstances to reject him even if he has every reason to feel totally assimilated. Feeling at ease or ill at ease in one's Jewishness cannot be equated with any other feelings of ease or disquiet a Jew may have; it comes on top of all the rest.

Here I am addressing the non-Jew devoid of anti-Jewish prejudice, who has nothing to forgive the Jews because he has nothing to reproach them with and is perfectly happy for them to be as they are. But what in fact are they? Are they what they would like to be or think they ought to be? Or what the non-Jewish world (from which I exclude the anti-Semites, who have already made up their minds) believes or wants them to be? We are obliged to infer the existence of a widespread preconceived image, difficult to eradicate, often difficult individually to detect, to which the non-Jew unconsciously expects Jews to conform. Because the image tends to be unflattering, the more liberal societies pride themselves on having a policy for the assimilation of Jews. Unfortunately, it rests on the unconscious assumption that nothing authentically Jewish in history, culture, and forms of self-expression can be of value. Furthermore, by denying the existence of one branch of the human family, assimilation impoverishes the parent tree by lopping off a branch.

Assimilation as so conceived is to apply to Jews alone. In the Soviet Union, a man can have "Jewish nationality" but be denied the cultural rights enjoyed, for instance, by a Uzbek. This is doubtlessly because Uzbek culture is as little known in Moscow as it is in Paris, London, or Washington—it is a matter for the scholar, of academic interest only—whereas Jewish culture (like the culture of the Kurds, as seen from Istanbul, Baghdad, or Teheran) is felt to be a menace. This is the crux of the problem.

Geography sets limits to national history and psychology and to people's ability to understand others. Hardly one Japanese in a hundred knows anything about the Passion of Christ, for instance, and the proportion of Europeans knowing anything about Shintoism would probably be even less, whereas among ten thousand Spaniards it would be hard to find one who has not retained at least some vague picture of the Passion story, from the Kiss of Judas to the Crucifixion. Curiosity and experience may enrich an individual existence, but our horizons are necessarily limited. Hence I speak essentially as an adult Jew whose life has been passed in the Mediterranean area—admittedly crucial for the history of mankind—and most of what I have to say will apply to this part of the world.

Within this area are to be found the two major ideological currents of our times: the civilizations of the Book derived from Judaism (firstly Christianity and latterly, largely for economic reasons, a more influential Islam), and Marxism, with its various deviant schools. These two major currents intermingle, coexist, or clash in circumstances such that Judaism is sometimes involved. Christian anti-Judaism began when the crime of deicide was imputed to a people for whom neither the word nor the crime could have any meaning. Throughout almost the whole of history, almost everywhere, murder has been the supreme crime and sin, for which the penalty was death. The murder of God was therefore the crime of crimes, a sin of unimaginable horror. Burdened for centuries with this awful charge, universally suspect, humiliated and sneered at, the Jews are only just beginning to emerge from the shadow. They have nevertheless remained faithful to a messianic hope in a progress both possible and desirable, to be achieved at the cost of constant effort, but totally unpredictable. Deaf to the appeals of the newer civilizations of the Book, Judaism, or the active principle in it—now embodied in a State—has remained inflexibly opposed to the rising tide of "progressive" ideologies, professedly atheistic or secular but in fact possessing many of the features of intense religious faith. Those who doubt whether the spirit of revelation exists in Marxism should consider the scope and implications of the following, eloquent in its confidence and concision: "Communism is the answer to the riddle of History and knows that it is that answer."[1] Whence a certain connivance, which may appear strange at first sight, between religions reputedly conservative and creeds which, though superficially secular, are in fact intensely religious in tone.

It is, however, not my intention to tamper with the preserve of faith. Rather, I wish to show that what is permanent and lasting in Judaism (this may have little relationship to the imaginings of those who stand outside Judaism) is at odds with new, triumphant religions and doctrines which, originally confident of bringing about heaven on earth, have now run into vicissitudes of their own creation.

The Undefinable

Having said enough about being a Jew in the world and the Jewish condition, I feel obliged, before going further, to attempt a definition of Jewishness. But except for legal and hence limited purposes, it is scarcely possible to define what one perceives to exist. A tree, a puddle, moonlight, the wind rising and falling—to define the emotion they arouse is to destroy it. Nor can one define that which is acquired by being experienced. To be Jewish is a fact of life—something given which I can convey only in general, inadequate terms, something to be lived, to be grasped, an inner richness which should be obvious to anyone who is not hostile to or afraid of life.

This groping approach to "becoming the person-you-are" (Nietzsche) explains why so many Jews caught up in a process of assimilation (both constraining and constantly liable to be challenged) feel ill at ease both in relation to Judaism and to the non-Jewish world, since they are not forging their own destiny but rather submitting to the inevitable as they see it. They neither face the facts and their own

[1] Karl Marx, *Manuscripts*, 1844.

experience nor take any risks, by taking part in a collective experience the roots of which are foreign to them. Part of the malaise experienced by the Jew is a reaction to the resentment felt by those not prepared to accept him as a Jew, or his right to live as such.

It is therefore not easy to define what is meant by being a Jew in the world (although the difficulty is often exaggerated by anti-Semites for their own purposes, as though the ambiguity were limited to Jews). We shall be on easier ground in defining Judaism. Here we shall no longer be concerned with isolated living beings, constantly interacting with the ideas which others have of them, but we shall try to grasp the nature of continuity as opposed to permanent movement and to isolate the quality which links them all together. Any definition we can give will be descriptive only, never exhaustive, and this is natural—how could one, for instance, define Switzerland in any other way?

Let us at any rate try. Judaism is first and foremost, of course, a *religion*, even if it is something else besides. We are thus inevitably faced with the concept of God, and I wish to define it within the context beyond which I do not wish to move, i.e., sociological, historical, and existential, without any definite religious connotations. In other words, I confine myself to the concepts or formulations that are the product of human consciousness. What then I understand by "God" is the justification, the motor, and the ideal which have enabled man to fashion his history or at any rate have helped him in so doing. I am well aware of the abuses to which this idea has given rise, but this is extraneous to my theme. Nor am I naive enough to believe that the mental life of man is totally independent of the social and economic conditions of the community in which he lives. But the creations of this mental life inevitably go beyond and sometimes challenge this socio-economic substructure, occasionally with dangerous results, and there is a particularly dangerous tendency to try to bring about the Kingdom of God upon earth, even though this may be at the expense of the dreamers themselves.

It is consciousness that enables man to escape from tribal segregation and to overcome chaos. It is man's greeting to light, recognized in Genesis as the first proof of a Supreme Being. It is already in the appeal "More Light!" said to have been Goethe's last words. As it evolves, the mental life of man develops and takes as many different forms as there are thinking individuals. But it goes counter to religious tradition only once it has detached itself from it and not always without upheavals. The secularization of Western Jewry in the last century was possible only because of and even in opposition to institutionalized Judaism.

However, to reduce Judaism to a religion, as the anti-Zionists try to do for political motives, is to mutilate it. When the anti-Zionist declares, with a feigned magnanimity, that of course the Jew will be free to profess his faith in a secular, democratic Palestine, what he means is that such a faith will be a purely private matter, tolerated as an inoffensive fossilized remnant of a religion in an Islamic or Marxist society. In the same way, Christianity is tolerated today in the Soviet Union provided it remains strictly confined to the four walls of a church. In this latter country, pious Jews are not even allowed the prayer books they want.

Tradition may not be purely religious. We have already had occasion to speak of Jewish universalism, with the generosity it demands and the dangers to which Jews are exposed as a result, and mentioned that the phenomenon is largely attributable to historical causes (successive migrations and the trauma of statelessness), whereas in the Bible and Talmud the election of the Jews and their universal vocation are interlocking themes.

In addition, Judaism implies the idea of *community*, without which religion and tradition would possess no constantly developing social infrastructure. Like every society, the Jewish community gives birth to various schools of thought and (unfortunately) creates its own red tape.

This community, or this collection of communities, clearly constitutes a *people*, first united, then dispersed, then to some extent regenerated, but always to some extent recognizably itself, even when possessed of the unrealizable idea of assimilation into some larger whole.

This community clearly has a *culture* of its own. But I prefer the term *civilization* as broader in scope. Littré's nineteenth-century French dictionary defines "civilization" thus: "Opinions and customs deriving from the reciprocal action of industry, religion, the arts and sciences." After centuries of fragmentation and imperfect liberty, Hebrew civilization meets this definition in part only. What is surprising is that after so long it should come so close to it. The Jews' achievement in this respect is indeed so remarkable that it is tempting to credit them with a mysterious quality placing them outside the normal rules of historical investigation—a temptation to which, as already indicated, I have no intention of yielding here.

To come back then to earth, Judaism can aptly be described as a *national ideology*; "ideology" as used in the Platonic sense of a theory of ideas and in the sense given to the expression by Raymond Aron: "An overall system for interpretation of historical and political realities." "National" because devoid of meaning when not founded on the nation, whether this exists in fact or is only an ideal. The concept of "nation"—not any nation but one attached to a given land (Eretz Israel)—is the theme which sustained Judaism over the centuries, irrespective of wherever the Jews happened to find themselves during the dispersion. Every spring at Passover, they pray: "Next year in Jerusalem!" All the historic feasts of the Hebrew calendar are connected with the tilling and sowing of land in that specific country or commemorate the events which marked the return to the Promised Land after the Egyptian exile, the desperate defence of that land by the Maccabees, or the tragedy of a "people scattered among the peoples" (Esther, III, 8).

Today, the Jewish people have reconstituted a *state* in the land of their ancestors. Here the anti-Zionist will sneeringly declare that there are more Jews outside Israel than in it. Certainly the volume and tempo of immigration has proved, for Zionists, disappointing; there are obstacles both external and internal to the undertaking, but it would be illegitimate to conclude that the latter is a mistake. Throughout the world, trade unions are not as powerful as the pioneers of the movement would have liked, but it does not follow that workers are mistaken in joining unions in defence of their interests. There are more Lebanese living abroad (even without counting the refugees produced by the civil war which broke out in 1975) than in Lebanon itself; nobody dreams of arguing from this that Lebanon as a country could be dispensed with. And the Lebanese living abroad would have less difficulty in readapting themselves to the conditions of their home country, whereas the Jews of the Diaspora still carry about with them the tinsel trappings acquired in centuries of wandering. It is facts that count, not potentialities, and there are today over three million Jews in Israel, more than the total population of Lebanon.

The above is merely an approach to the question. Now let us try to inquire into the deeper reasons for the great difficulty encountered by Judaism in making its voice heard.

"Hear, O Israel—the Lord our God, the Lord is One!"[2] First, a stubborn monotheism, a perpetual turning towards a Fullness-of-Being to the existence of which Judaism is an obstinate witness. Not that there have been no temptations, backslidings, or surrenders to force. But Judaism, by sheer tenacity, has somehow survived.

[2] Apart from the classical works on monotheism, there are some interesting and very personal views on Jewish "monolatry" to be found in Arnold Mandel, *Nous autres Juifs* ("We Jews"), Hachette, Paris.

The same is doubtless true of other religions and of various ideologies held with the force of a religious creed. Here, too, saints and martyrs and lives of quiet piety abound. None of these creeds has so long and so successfully resisted dispersion and oppression as Judaism. Politically impotent, the Jews have displayed an extraordinary religious tenacity. It can be argued that the one explains the other and that political alienation is the price to be paid for religious vitality. Personally, I cannot admit that perpetual sacrifices should be demanded of any community, especially when those sacrifices happen to be in the interests of others. However that may be, isolation within dominant majorities has led to a double current among Jews. On the one hand, there are those who fall away, are converted or assimilated into the non-Jewish majority; over the centuries this has represented an immense loss to the parent stem. On the other hand, there has been this extraordinary persistence in an intransigent monotheism:

> The Jew seems obsessed by the religious dimension to existence, by the "fact" of God. Whatever he may do—close his ears, swear that he hears nothing—the words: "I Am That I Am" remain imprinted on his soul. He has received a message. He can do what he likes with it. But he is a Jew by virtue of that message and of what he intends to do with it.[3]

We are dealing, then, with individuals and communities which have remained true to themselves in the shifting sands of history, tenaciously bearing a divine message. It was for me a deeply moving experience to meet, in Delhi, a tiny group of men and women (twenty or so, the women in saris)—the last survivors of an ancient Jewish community which had somehow survived the various tides (Christian, Moslem, Buddhist, Hindu) which have swept over this part of the world. The Jews seem to be invested with a universal mission; they are, in very truth, a *particular* people with a *world-wide* message. Such a vocation is burdensome at times.

"But he is a Jew by virtue of that message and of what he intends to do with it." What in fact does he do? Here again, we encounter an astonishing thing—the absolute value attached by Judaism to the finite human being, depository of the divine message and responsible for spreading it. Precarious, vulnerable, human life is sacred.

[3] Francois Fejtö, *Dieu et son Juif* ("God and His Jew"), Grasset, Paris.

Other religions transfer their absolute values into the personal or collective hereafter (if not into death itself). But the Old Testament contains no trace of any explicit belief in an afterlife. The Jew is responsible here and now. If he fails, there will be neither punishment nor rehabilitation in a life to come. All he knows—if he believes—is that the mission he has to accomplish in this life adds to the sacred character of the latter.

The same in the last resort applies to even the most secularized Jew. It is in this sense that we can legitimately point to the messianism present in Marx. This is why we find so high a proportion of "non-Jewish" Jews, self-styled, in the van of every movement for reform and revolution. Such persistence in trying to bring about a better world here and now is a curious characteristic, and in a non-Jewish world has brought down a lot of trouble on Jewish heads.

What is striking about mainstream Judaism is the steadfast refusal to seek consolation in the hereafter. For the Jew, salvation from the sins and wickedness of this world lies in the messianic hope of a better life here below.

The Talmud tells the story of Rabbi Jochanan ben Zakkai, famous for his wisdom. One day, while he was digging in his garden, some peasants passed by and called to him cheerfully: *"What are you doing there, Rabbi? Do you not know that the Messiah has come?"* "Where?" *"In the village square."* The sage stopped digging for a moment and took his time before replying: *"I shall go presently."* "Why not now, Rabbi?" *"I must finish this work first."* Like all Talmudic stories, this one lends itself to an infinity of interpretations. I interpret it as meaning that the Messiah will not come until such time as all of us, wise as well as foolish, have finished the tasks assigned to us. The Rabbi knows that his garden can wait, that nothing obliges him to go on digging, and that it would be more important to greet the Messiah. But he knows, too, that this is impossible in the circumstances.

Observe, too, that if the Rabbi, having done his day's work, had run into the village and found that the news, or the Messiah, had been false, he would have gone back to his garden. He would have sought no consolation. The Messiah is the opposite of Father Christmas; we cannot ever be sure when he will come.

Judaism is therefore a severe, a difficult faith, and those who prefer religions which promise rewards on earth or in heaven may find its demands impossible. The kind of revelation offered by these other faiths may act as a bait and a spur. But should they be left behind by events, they are faced with the need for a face-lift.

Edenism, Ethics, and History

From the above we have seen that Judaism is "different" in a different way, and therefore specially troublesome and intrusive, particularly for those religions which are united, despite their differences, in justifying suffering by reference to some Absolute Beatitude to be attained either in the hereafter or on earth. This aspiration and the myths deriving therefrom seem to survive the constant progress of science and technology, and the anaesthesia induced by the affluent society. In the Christian West, life here and now has traditionally faded before the glories awaiting the individual soul in the world to come; in the Communist East, salvation will take the form of rising social standards here on earth. The result is what I call Edenism—a determined, even if unconscious, attempt to bring about a world in which dreams will coincide with history, plus the optimism required to believe that such a thing is possible. Edenists believe that they have left Judaism behind, but its very survival is felt as a kind of affront. Jewish scepticism about pie-in-the-sky has to be paid for by persecution, attempts at assimilation, or condescension.

Even when Judaism cannot possibly be to blame, history and ethics do not follow the same path. The newly independent countries offer an unhappy example; morally, they are no better, and sometimes worse, than the systems which preceded them. There is no necessary coincidence between the possible and what appears necessary, and this the Edenists will not acknowledge. Since history has a sense—the sense they give it—such coincidence *must* exist. When they see that history refuses to obey the laws of a morality they have projected onto it, they think not of changing the morality but of altering the course of events. The saboteurs of history, those who divert it from the course it should take, are always in the other camp. We shall then have show-trials, executions, and so on; history is full of such things, although in the end surprisingly little changes. In the meantime, a disastrous balance-sheet will be presented as a pledge of a radiant future. "Tomorrow you will be able to have a free shave," say those who, razor in hand, have already done some throat-slitting. In the name of a political dream, they do not hesitate to chastise history for indocility. Should they have read Hegel, they will be able to quote him: "So much the worse for facts."

Edenism is therefore essentially unrealistic and unrealizable. At all times there has been in Christianity a strain of other-worldliness, a radical rejection of this world and a belief that life here below is but a preparation of the life to come. More surprisingly, we find apostles of historical materialism who are prisoners of their own dreams and mental projections, separated from life, like the religious Edenists, by their own preconceptions and content to postpone the millennium to an indefinite future. The Inquisitors saw nothing wrong in burning bodies to save souls. Today, in the name of an idealized "secular Palestine" in which Jews are to live in peace and amity with their neighbours, living Jews are cheerfully slain. Similarly, in February 1943, at a time when the Germans were deporting Jews from France by the trainload, a "Francist" weekly (Francism was a French fascist movement whose members cooperated with the Germans) drew a distinction "between the Jew (man, woman or child) of whom France would be well rid, and his immortal soul which the Creator, in His infinite mercy, can save."

In all these cases, the survival of the Jews is a refutation of that eschatological view of things which history has so obviously condemned, including the high hopes once entertained of the 1917 Revolution. Hence, anti-Semitism is in no sense a feature of the Right alone.

Messianism—Its Moral Force and Political Weakness

Since man makes history, he can also change it. A revolt such as that of the Warsaw ghetto proved, if proof were needed, that rebellion, no matter how forlorn, is not necessarily pointless. Whether victorious or vanquished, the passively oppressed becomes the active rebel. But nothing the rebel can do will enable him to influence the state of mind which derives moral comfort from oppression. It is more realistic to wish to change the world than to hope for the conversion of the Nuremberg accused to a philosophy of humanism.

Unless the persecutor decides to stop persecuting because he has felt something. But what? I cannot say exactly, but perhaps this is what is meant by the messianic hope—a faith in man from which the enemies of man cannot exclude themselves, as Anne Frank said just before being led off to her death by such enemies. Such a faith is the contrary of a subjective delirium, since even when, for the sake of self-preservation, the enemy has to be done to death, it is ultimately based on faith in him as a man like any other. For someone animated by such a faith, to change history does not imply changing men from outside and by force; one day, he believes, men will be able to change it by virtue of their inner force.

To some extent the Jews have always lived under the sign of the messianic hope. To some extent only, because at no time in history have all Jews been fully aware of the responsibilities entailed. Some have not been aware at all; I think of those who worshipped the Golden Calf, or the anti-Zionist, alienated Jews of today. In between we have that Spanish sixteenth-century rabbi Shlomo Halevi, who became a Christian, then Bishop of Burgos and a pitiless persecutor of Jews. There are many Jews such as these, not lucid enough to realize just how much of the messianic hope lies, in a perverted form, at the root of the attempts they make to obliterate their indebtedness to Judaism. But their enemies are rarely mistaken. They know that Jewish history, for all its ups and downs, remains marked by adhesion to a hope which is both its strength and its weakness. It is the Jew's weak point, his Achilles heel, but at the same time the diamond which by its glitter offends and alarms his enemies.

The political weakness of Judaism derives from its very nature. When the enemies of the Jewish nation take Israeli hostages to blackmail the government in Jerusalem, they know full well that this government is stronger than they and would not hesitate, if it were as brutal and ruthless as they proclaim, to take ten Arab hostages for every Jew (as the Germans did in occupied Europe) and then use them to secure the release of the Israeli hostages. But Israel's enemies also know that such methods will never be adopted, even though Israelis be forced to watch, in impotent rage, the murder of their own flesh-and-blood. The enemies of Israel know full well that however odious their behaviour, there are certain depths to which Israel will not stoop. This is a case in which moral strength becomes political weakness.

An Open Eschatology

Christian and Islamic Edenisms derive their strength from their promises for the future. Marxism does the same, though careful to invoke scientific causality; the proletariat, progressively shrinking, as Marxist principles deteriorate, to the party, then to the Politburo, and finally to the leader, is the predestined agent of revolutionary change, the automatic victor in the class struggle, and finally the force which will create a classless society. Jewish thought by comparison seems very down-to-earth. But it is realistic in so far as its ends remain undefined and its ideals without limits. Its philosophy in practical terms becomes: "Do what you have to do, come what may." Sow the seed, plant the tree. Behave as though your task has to be completed and well completed, as though the tree must bear only the most splendid fruit. If the tree languish because of drought, if it be damaged by hail, look after it. If destroyed by fire or swept away by flood, or if it give poisoned fruit, plant another. Ceaselessly begin again, renew, pursue the daily round, the common task. And with no belief in reward. Not merely because good action is its own reward, but because it is the bearer of hope.

Edenism takes various forms in an attempt to mitigate the endless wait for the millennium. One form affirms that there is a solution to life's problems and claims to possess it; another merely considers that a solution *must* exist. Perhaps it is not being overly pessimistic to assert that this is not necessarily true. And that while some of man's activities as a social being may be bad (or, to avoid the language of ethics, let us say "dangerous" for himself and society), it is not certain that there is any cure. Nor is it certain that curative action might not degenerate into something worse. Doubtless something has to be done to ward off evil and face up to danger. But to recommend that an attempt be made is very different from seeking to impose a solution, which is what some of the forms of Edenism which dominate our society attempt to do. My scepticism is at least based on the bitter lessons of history.

The history of society, like the lives of men, is subject to ups and downs rendered easier to bear by dreams of a better future, as Marxist critics have vigorously asserted in their criticism of the traditional religions, overlooking the fact that Marxism, too, is open to the same charge.

On the other hand, Judaic messianism, as vaguely imagined and feared (although in this century at any rate Jewish thought seems to have produced little to justify such fears), represents a point of departure at which nothing is given or taken for granted, a point beyond which anything is possible providing illusion and self-deception are rigorously eschewed, for "life is not a perpetual examination leading to the award of a diploma for eternal life, but an element in which the spirit moves and has its being."[4] The least failing jeopardizes all that has so far been achieved. Dreams are excluded, and ideological ones all the more so. If all of them fail, so much the worse; we shall simply have to wait. In the meantime, we must learn to do without them. It is significant that the realities of Israel are denied by the dream world in which so many heads of state and leaders of thought delight. It is deplorable that there should be Jews to lend their support to such lack of realism by maintaining that Jewry would welcome its own destruction.

[4] Emmanuel Levinas, *Difficile liberté* ("Difficult Freedom"), Albin Michel, Paris.

Edenists become the more aggressive the more they are challenged by uncomfortable realities. They then seek refuge in war or terrorism, commit intellectual suicide, or seek absorption in the affluent society.

The road to paradise demands a guide, leader, or guru who will direct, protect, and reassure, a Duce or a Mao or both together, as with those tiny Italian groups which claim to be of the extreme Left and far Right at the same time. The shepherd being infallible, any mistakes he may make in guiding his flock, and anything disagreeable which may occur within it, will be the responsibility of the sheep themselves.

The disciple once lost is bewildered, fearful of abandonment, afraid of loss of faith. Is paradise out of reach or even unimaginable? The prospect is almost too awful to be faced. Happily the shepherd has foreseen everything, including the possibility that individual lambs may go astray. Although the disciple may have lost his way, he still believes that paradise exists. Perhaps he himself was to blame for losing his bearings; certainly, he would like to believe this, for there is nothing so uncomfortable as to be lost, not to be one of the flock, to be like the Jews, whose fate it is not to belong to the herd, who unnervingly proclaim that paradise does not exist, or that the time for it is not yet come, and there is no sure recipe for bringing it about.

Despite an irresistible tendency to make projections into the future, Edenists tend to look over their shoulders as well. Some claim that the Messiah has already come, although the world seems to have little to show for it. Or paradise is projected into a world-to-come, and the disciples will then have to qualify for entry by deeds in this life. Others make a myth of an event in the past (the 1917 Revolution is a case in point). The myth then serves as a pretext for all sorts of exactions in the name of a glorious future.

Edenism goes naturally with a belief in demons, for Hell is needed to accommodate those unworthy of Heaven, and especially the heretics who doubt the existence of both. For Judaism, the Beyond—Heaven and Hell—does not with any certainty exist. Monotheism is already a form of Messianism since it implies a permanent turning towards a single God. The Kingdom of God is to be brought about here below, by rendering the possible present here and now, by the faithful accomplishment of human tasks on a human scale by the whole of mankind. The idolaters who invest an image of the Kingdom of God with their own mental projections feel that messianism makes superhuman demands on human nature. In fact, such demands go no further than what one man can expect of his own capacities or of anyone else. Judaism, in asking men to do without dreams and visions, makes a bet on their ability to fend for themselves.

Certain events—the Crucifixion, the fire at the El-Aqsa Mosque, the "doctors' plot" which Jewish doctors in the Soviet Union were accused of having fomented against Stalin just before his death—have acquired a symbolic significance and a powerful emotional charge, especially when non-Edenists (i.e., the Jews) were held responsible. In all three cases, they have defiled a major symbol. Should a handful of them have the unparalleled audacity to pray on what was, after all, the site of the Temple (mosques having been erected there only very much later), passions at once run riot.

The very attitude of expectation characteristic of Judaism becomes an aggravating circumstance, since it seems to imply refusal to recognize a firmly established tradition. The charge of deicide, still very much alive in the Christian conscience, especially among Christian anti-Zionists, is aggravated in men's minds by the thought that God's assassins are sacrilegiously awaiting a Messiah other than Christ, thus challenging the central tenets of the Christian faith. *Mutatis mutandis*, a similar charge is brought against the Jews by those for whom the emergence of Mohammed (or of the Marxist State) represents a turning point in history. True, the image is no longer one of the bloody death of God Himself on the Cross, as passed on from generation to generation. Nevertheless, the image persists of an Israel stubbornly pursuing a path of its own, insensitive to the ends of history.

Hence the Edenists, so apt, once the emotion has died away, to lose interest in the dramas of their own history, are exceedingly interested in that tiny part of the earth's surface where the Jews are effectively free. This interest readily turns into an obsession, the freedom to be Jewish becomes some dark Jewish plot to achieve "world domination." How absurd this is becomes apparent if we consider what happened in Poland, where a handful of Jews, survivors of the greatest massacre in history, perpetrated by Poland's greatest enemy, have been accused of being either too Stalinist or insufficiently so, to suit the convenience of the Polish government.

Commitment and Humanism

Judaism is also an awkward customer in that it allows of no swings from one pole to another. The blame for infirmity of purpose or for frustration can be laid at nobody else's door. Judaism does not allow of the dichotomy which obtains between humanism and commitment, whereby so many on the Left can denounce torture and injustice only when committed by the Right (and vice versa). It represents *a commitment to humanism.*

But there is nothing abstract or subjective about such a humanism. It is a historical process. What is lived at this very moment is total existence not merely because it is the only present but because it determines the future. While, for Jewish thought, God is at the beginning and end of the road, it is the road itself which gives meaning to the life of man.

Nor can a man's life be an individual adventure, to be crowned with the approval of society or of God in the form of a decoration or an absolution. The messianic outlook embodies the sum total of each man's ventures in the course of his life. The messianic era is just within grasp and yet always elusive. As a grain of dust can pollute a glass of water, so a single impurity of will can annul the best of intentions. The slightest setback jeopardizes the equilibrium of the world, which then becomes chaotic, or at best imperfect. If I change, I must in so doing help to change the world. But no change, even if it be a world revolution, can change anything in me unless I have freely wished it to do so. (For instance, I am certain that the first free inquiry to be undertaken in China will show how insubstantial and ultimately uninfluential was the cult of the thought of Mao.) This being so, a commitment of this kind goes beyond anything human imagination can conceive of, reaching out for a cosmos to which even the cosmonauts have no access.

Not so easy. So, to continue to believe, tricks have to be invented. We have to suppose that a force external to ourselves can make good our weaknesses and failings. For the Marxist Edenist, this will be the course of history itself, with its irreversible, implacable dialectic. For the Christian, it will be effective grace or the will of God. Both schools of thought criticize Islam for fatalism. Both demand continuous cooperation from the subject, who no longer has any reason for impatience since his own commitment coincides with the "Promise of History" or the "Divine Pledge." Both vividly describe a future in which the faithful will be rewarded for their pains—a kind of supreme historical provident fund, called upon to offer compensation for the sins, shortcomings, and failures of the world we know.

We are, however, not so distant from the original source as we might imagine. Hence those who proclaim that the young student rebels in the Paris of May 1968 were manipulated by "Zionists" so as to make things difficult for the pro-Arab policies of General de Gaulle are perhaps not so far as might be believed from a truth which obviously they do not see. Alas, all rebels find this out for themselves; man can be sure of nothing, and certainly not of paradise. Judaism demands that a man perform the daily round, the common task, and then make a further effort over and above that. If the hope be total, the effort must be so also. If it be believed that the hope will be realized, the effort made is rewarded in advance.

From time to time we behold the emergence of crests which point the way to a higher stage in the development of mankind. The ancient Jewish prophets, among others, mark the way. And how Jewish in this context is the marvelous adventure of Jesus! It ceased to be Jewish when the prophet and hero of a world in gestation was turned into a symbol of sanctity to be acquired by self-sacrifice. After the Apostle Paul, the Church will make good use of the blood shed by the Christ; its priests, scribes, and artists will unite to create a vision in which the image of suffering flesh-and-blood produces in the believer a sense of guilt and a hope of expiation for that guilt. The historical materialists intervene here to recall that the ideal community of paradise is to be brought about here on earth. Of course, they add, one or two generations will have to be sacrificed; paradise will certainly not be here the day after tomorrow.

Edenists are, as it were, nostalgic for the future. They are already licking their lips at the thought of a future which resembles a fine old wine certified by the supreme authority: "Not to be drunk for . . . years." For Judaism, there is no millennium, and it is almost certain that there will be no paradise for me. The future is not to be sought in the stars or in any form of revelation; it is that which cannot by nature be revealed. In the darkness through which we stumble, one spark will cast no light, but millions of sparks perhaps might. I therefore have to make my own contribution, however modest. In this, Albert Camus, poles apart from traditional Judaism, is not as far as one might think from its ethic.

Judaism is above all else a code of ethics around which is built up a faith, not the other way round. It is so saturated with ethical considerations that nobody can be sure of absolution from his sins and failings, and nobody can absolve someone else. Even God cannot absolve. "A fault committed with regard to God can be pardoned only by God; one involving an offence to man is not a matter for God's pardon."[5] The dead do not rise to pardon the living.

But every Edenistic faith provides for absolution of the sinner and rehabilitation

---

[5] E. Levinas, *op. cit.*, with reference to the Talmud.

of the offender, so that with assistance from the priest or party secretary there is always hope of regaining Paradise Lost. Such an operation can generally be done, but only for a consideration. And it is thought to be profitable. I do not wish to underestimate the Christian or Marxist eschatologies, the moral ambitions and demands of which are undeniable. For the believing Christian or convinced Marxist, life must be one long succession of agonizing questions about the gulf between faith and works. Absolution or rehabilitation ought never to be sufficient, but in the world as it is, alas, they suffice only too easily. The politicians of church or party, knowing how far men can go in seeking accommodation with themselves, take advantage of this knowledge and enjoy almost unlimited freedom of maneuver. But who, in the last resort, are taken in if not men?

In the battle for absolute justice which will herald the messianic era, no accommodation is possible. The superhuman efforts demanded of me are possible in one direction only, with no chance of slipping from one set of rails to another, and with no witness other than the Eye which pursued Cain to the tomb. How awkward a thing is conscience, revealing false motives for what they are, ignoring routine, refusing to be washed away by psychoanalysis, suspicious of rapture, not fearing reduction to the sacred, making nonsense of theories, ever present and ready to bring the well-oiled machine of self-justification to a standstill. The most fearful thing of all is that it exists. In each of us, in Cain himself. A man whose ways of thinking have been fashioned by the religions of the Book will despite himself always retain a certain ambiguity in his views on Judaism. Awareness of the fact that the more recent religions of the Book have been guilty in their attitude to Judaism may be transmuted into straightforward anti-Judaism, and a man will set his conscience at rest by discovering all the reasons there may be to dislike the Jews. Or an uneasy conscience may adopt some degree of pro-Judaism which at its best is identifiable with humanism. Most people fall uneasily between the two positions. Their pro-Judaism is condescending; while willing to protect the Jew against his enemies (many Christians, Moslems, and secular democrats have displayed courage in so doing), such people are above all concerned to protect him against himself; the ultimate, unavowed, or half-explicit aim being to reduce him to the status of a non-Jew. Should the Jew, however, no longer wish to remain the eternal victim or *protégé* and want to assume responsibility for his own fate, then everything is called in question.

Mental Imagery

It is therefore no accident that anti-Zionism is so hard to eradicate. It cannot readily be reduced to a clash of nationalities, or explained away by economic interests, or the class struggle, or political options, although it may ally itself with one or the other. A problem such as that of the Malayan Chinese embodies all these factors; it is not easy to settle and has already cost enough in blood and tears. But neither the Chinese in Malaysia nor the Malays would dream of employing in relation to each other the kind of language currently used against Israel.

Anti-Zionism may take insidious forms in which the underlying hatred is masked and the thought warped to an absurd degree, as when an international congress can solemnly declare that Zionism is prejudicial to the emancipation of women. When the Israeli delegate at that congress said that the dominant majority was just as likely to rule that the earth was flat, something more than a bitter joke was involved. If a motion to this effect is not passed, this is simply because the dominant majority has no interest in securing its adoption. But we are already living in a world whose unity (in a sense its roundness) is denied.

Today the classical Right with some liberal leanings is less openly opposed to a renovated Judaism as embodied in Israel for reasons readily understood. The Right has never believed in a Kingdom of God on earth and feels totally unconcerned in the efforts made to bring it about. Messianism, as the Right sees it, is of no political consequence. Nevertheless, should it suspect a Jew of taking an active part in any political movement, it relapses all too readily into an anti-Semitism of the traditional kind. Furthermore, little given to political analysis other than superficial, it tends automatically to assume that might is right.

On the other hand, the fascist extreme Right, reactionary and "Edenistic" in so far as it champions traditional values to be embodied in some New Order, is more inclined to anti-Zionism in that it offers a new target for latent anti-Semitism. Fascism is a primitive and short-sighted form of Edenism; it needs no ideology, which is replaced by a self-sufficient cult of violence and by the mystique of a charismatic leader. Younger than either Christianity or Marxism, fascist Edenism takes over, and exaggerates, their totalitarian tendencies, deliberately overlooking the humanistic aspects of these two faiths.

Radical left-wing Edenism, on the other hand, believing it has a monopoly claim to radicalism, willingly takes over fascist values—violence, a taste for destruction, an inability to think dialectically, an overweening contempt for liberalism, humanism, and similar values—making use of arguments borrowed from the "revolutionary" Left, although such arguments have become a currency so depreciated that even the extreme Right does not hesitate to borrow them on occasion.

When carried to these extremes, Edenism feels the imperious need to set itself over against a distorted image of the one country where Jews are free, the Palestinian being elevated into the role of the liberator whose sacred duty it is to extirpate the bedraggled Zionist dragon. This is easily done by making two artificial distinctions. The first is between the Jews and Israel (the Judaism left over being no more than an empty shell), and then all anti-Jewish prejudices are transferred wholesale to this detestable country in the name of contemporary trendy causes: anti-imperialism, enthusiasm for the Third World, etc. The second is between the *fedayeen* and the Arabs; in this manner, the *fedayeen* remain untainted by those more disagreeable features of the contemporary Arab world which are too glaringly obvious to be excused or explained away: hysteria, megalomania, corruption, feudalism, police repression, etc. For people who argue in this way, any government created in Palestine by the PLO would be different, the Palestinians being of course able to put into effect the excellent intentions with which they are credited. They thus embody the historical miracle to which these Edenists transfer the hopes (now unfortunately dashed) once invested in the workers of the affluent society or in the newly independent, poverty-stricken peoples of the Third World.

People who think like this will cast the runes against Israel. They will try to persuade themselves that not only has this country no right to exist (and most certainly no right to be strong or victorious), it has no *reason* to exist either.

Anti-Jewish obscurantism has never been one of those stagnant ponds which in the end dry up. Its underlying Edenism gives it a kind of life—putrid perhaps but in continual lazy movement. Ideas and images become degraded. Thus, in bygone centuries, a Jew could earn a living only by dealing in money; then his wealth was seized and he was laid under a curse (observe that this took place only when the owner or lender of money was a Jew); later still it was asserted that Jews were by nature miserly, close-fisted, etc., and could be nothing else. Transpose this to the spiritual level. Firstly, it is decided that Jewry can exist only in a "religious" sense (as affirmed in the Palestinian Charter,[6] a document reflecting a typically

---

[6]To my mind, successfully demolished by Robert Misrahi in *La Philosophie politique et l'Etat d'Israël*, Editions Mouton, The Hague-Paris, and Y. Harkabi, *op. cit.*

colonialist approach). Then we are told that such a community, being "theocratic," is somehow detestable. Finally, the Jewish people, alone among the peoples of this part of the world (none of which is "secular"), must be destroyed because their community is not a secular one.

Apart from a handful of the more thoughtful students of Islamic affairs, anti-Zionists grant the Palestinians no more than a shadowy existence as a necessary backdrop for their mental imagery. The Palestinians are thus relegated to perpetual insecurity and permanent aggressive opposition to their one potential ally. Assuredly, an Israeli-Palestinian alliance would not be easy to bring about. But it is not inconceivable, and it would be in the interests of both parties. Anti-Zionism claims to be a friend of the Arab peoples; in fact, it holds them back by fostering those elements in Arab culture which make for stagnation and regression. It pays an unworthy tribute to terrorism, adulated because of—not in spite of—the suffering it causes. May the Palestinians one day realize they are being used and turn against their—our—common foe.

The Avatars of the Sacred

The opposition between Judaism and Edenisms makes itself felt in the irrational nature of many of the accusations regularly launched against Israel. Thus a condemnation of ritual murder, together with anathema passed on the Jews for deicide and a call to Holy War—all these are ideas underlying the judgments passed on the Israeli defence forces. In the event of a clash between these forces and the enemies of Israel, with casualties on both sides, an anti-Zionist will sometimes forget the Israeli dead or welcome the fact that there should have been so many. The "victims" who win all the sympathy are the Arabs. That Arabs may have lost their lives is never ascribed to the fortunes of war, still less to Arab obstinacy in waging war on Israel. The Israeli State is always guilty, believing neither in Christ nor in the Holy Prophet, nor in Marxism as the highest stage in human thought. I am, it is true, deliberately exaggerating to make a point which might otherwise pass unnoticed. In any event, I maintain that if other motives cannot be found, then these are likely to have been present, and that very often, if other motives exist as well, the ones I mention here are likely to gain the upper hand. Thus Arabs killed by Israelis can never, for the anti-Zionist, be the unhappy victims of an unfortunate conflict (although he will reason like that about the Lebanese civil war, in which all parties are Arab). They are heroes deliberately assassinated by the forces of evil, as in the Middle Ages Christian infants were said to have been sacrificed by perfidious and bloodthirsty Jews.

Observe, too, the speechless indignation which seems to overcome so many atheists and agnostics at the idea that a Jewish State—of all things—could actually be in control of the Christian and Islamic holy places. The charge that Israel is a "theocracy" is absurdly wide of the mark, and in any case the expression is much more aptly used of the Islamic countries. What in fact worries the anti-Zionist is not the fate of such-and-such a mosque or church (the West indeed has been indifferent for centuries) but rather that Jewish religious fervour should remain one of the springs of Jewish national resurrection.

Another form of dishonesty is to feign surprise that Judaism (in its political form as Zionism) should object and that Jews should refuse to be done to death. Moreover, the religions of the Book, offsprings of Judaism, involve themselves in contradiction in refusing to allow the Jews their part in God's designs. Such a refusal can be justified only in terms of religions placing the Jews within a conceptual scheme according to which, while being the Chosen People, they are nevertheless damned.

Only a completely secular outlook can recognize the Jewish sense of the sacred as being a historical phenomenon bound up with a certain culture or way of life and in no way a threat to other societies possessing their own sense of the sacred. Among the non-secular societies, which constitute the immense majority on earth today, only those entirely foreign to Judaism, and hence to the religions of the Book, can take an attitude of complete detachment towards Judaism—a detachment as complete as that with which we view the religion of the Incas. For Christian and Moslem thought (and this holds good of Marxism, too, in so far as it has messianic claims), refusal to recognize the validity of what Jews hold sacred is all too often a defence of their own religious values, including an inclination to attribute to Judaism an aggressiveness they refuse to recognize in themselves.

A *Permanent Challenge*

Many faiths offer men an escape from fate. Judaism here is weak, offering no easy way out—neither an inaccessible summit nor an abyss in which to plunge. It maintains no more than a flickering flame of hope and does nothing to nourish it. For those who feel the need for a light on their way, this meagre illumination does not suffice.

The messianic perspective will have no commerce with a promise of reward so definite as to be a constraint on man's freedom. It is more precarious in that it is total and can be totally gained or lost. Such freedom is continually being tested and challenged. It alone allows of effective action on the outside world. But a world dominated by fear is afraid of freedom. Believers in other creeds will step in to exploit the gap left by Judaism, offering the reassurance that fear and weakness demand. Who can blame them? Let the man who thinks of himself as strong and claims not to know what fear of the unknown means cast the first stone.

Sometimes, however, fear will no longer be held in check and the need for reassurance has at all costs to be satisfied. To this end, some ready-made formula will be invented and then a judgment becomes legitimate. Jean Paul Sartre was once asked by a journalist for a brief definition of existentialism. His answer was that in man existence preceded essence, whereas the reverse was true of a pickled cucumber. I quote his statement because the man-made recipe is the enemy of freedom. But there may be several ways of serving a pickled cucumber; there is no sure recipe for human happiness, and least of all a formula, whether scientific or magical. This basic point is not usually admitted, perhaps because it costs an effort to make the admission.

Is Judaism serene or troubled, confidently certain or tragically uncertain? Perhaps all these predicates hold true. One thing it is not, does not claim to be, and cannot be, and that is a recipe. The forces which propose recipes and derive their strength from so doing cannot accept any challenge to their science or their magic and in times of crisis will react by trying to destroy the source from which the challenge comes. They all hold Judaism guilty of whatever they see, or think they see, in it. Should it appear serene and patient, this is taken as incorrigible scepticism; if disquieting, this is a sign of some dangerous heresy. In any event, its mere existence is for them a constant challenge to the truth they claim to represent. Judaism is a permanent challenge by man to himself. It is a challenge which may give rise to fears of a far more dangerous kind than those of the weak, who can be consoled and led, since these are fears felt by the leaders themselves (leader = *Führer* in German; *Vojd* in Russian, the term Stalin used in his heyday; *Imam* in contemporary Iran). The fears also felt, sometimes more acutely, by their subordinates or imitators.

For all of them, the heretic represents heresy, which they can apprehend only in having the heretic at their mercy. In this fashion, men, women, and those near and dear to them can be humiliated, persecuted, made to disappear. Their belongings can be confiscated or destroyed. The dead can be dishonoured even in the tomb. An attempt may even be made, though it will never be entirely successful, to consign all heretical books to the flames. But against the heretical thought itself, though caricatured until it is almost unrecognisable, the tyrant is helpless. The idea itself makes its own way because it is not understood and cannot be stopped by the leaders and their henchmen. It is then embodied, in deliberately distorted form, into an ideology, whence it is transferred to a group and finally to individuals held to represent that group. This is what normally happens when strangers or foreigners are feared. Thus we slip by imperceptible stages from messianism to Judaism, then to Jewry, then to the Jews, and then to any particular Jew, although he may have almost nothing Jewish about him.

Fear leads to terror or panic only when the victim of such fear feels himself to be in a position of inferiority, and usually only briefly. Should it last, and should those who experience it be in a position to make their will felt, it turns into suspicion and mistrust. Basically irrational, it cannot be given conceptual form and is therefore projected on to anybody felt to be a challenge to the deeply held conviction. It then becomes all the easier to pick out a Jewish face, because he who does the selection has only the vaguest idea of what underlies his fears.

If, then, the very existence of Israel is felt by some to be an aggression, it is because the affirmation of a Jewish existence is felt to be an aggression by the eschatological faiths deriving from Judaism. For them, Jewish emancipation, as soon as it goes beyond demanding that toleration which is the maximum that can be allowed, represents an intolerable provocation. Any freedom to return to the deeper sources radically challenges (although in a form not very clearly understood) the diluted and composite rivulets which spring therefrom.

Fear in Its Various Forms and Its Essential Identity

The threat thus imagined to exist is out of all proportion to the actual power wielded by the Jews and is magnified whenever any country or authority feels itself directly challenged, even when the challenge arises in absolute independence of the Jews. In August 1968, the invasion of Czechoslovakia was justified by the Soviet Union, directly responsible, and by Arab imperialism, which gave its blessing to the operation, as a response to the "Zionist" threat to that unhappy country. Absurd though this clearly is, it is significant that a motive such as this was thought plausible enough for public opinion to swallow. At the time when Stalin, towards the end of his life, had become a rabid anti-Zionist, the French journalist J. M. Domenach could write: "It is all too obvious that the little State of Israel is no serious threat to the Soviet bloc. But the terrestrial hope represented by Zionism is an intolerable challenge."[7] I would add that the hope was not merely terrestrial and that the challenge was not to the Soviet bloc alone.

As soon as the external menace seems to abate, the fear is set to rest and the consequences it had entailed cease to exist. In such circumstances, institutional form may even be given to toleration of the Jews. But toleration is always precarious and can at any time be revoked; it is never a wholehearted recognition. The rebirth of Israel has upset somewhat the old process whereby there were swings from persecution to condescension and vice versa. During the early years of Israel's existence, some compensation was even offered for past injustices and persecutions, for which other countries felt a certain guilt. Only after the Six-Day War of June 1967 was the rebirth of Israel vaguely felt to present a threat, simply because a free Jewish State had been capable of defending itself and hitting back. It was therefore labelled "aggressive," and its enemies have gone on considering it potentially so despite all the reverses it could have suffered—indeed, would have suffered if they had had their way.

But at the nadir of their fortunes the Zionist Jews had grasped the fact that their freedom and their continued existence were inseparable. In 1945, the Jews had one choice only, namely, to go on depending on the good will of others or to seek their freedom. It was impossible to go on passively awaiting the Messiah; a nation had to be created. Thus was Israel reborn.

After the attempts (very nearly successful) to annihilate them entirely, Jews feel that any return to the old relation of dependence mixed with condescension is unimaginable. Any argument justifying such a return or calling for it is legally indefensible, politically wretched, and humanly monstrous. Is it really possible to imagine the survivors who arrived in Israel in the least seaworthy of ships, or were returned to the German camps still full of the smell of death, wondering and worrying about whether or not they should go back—and where to?

Among those not directly concerned, who have not fallen into the anti-Zionist trap, the most thoughtful have realized that their own freedom and that of the world would be at stake if they were to refuse the Jews, and them alone, their freedom. It matters little whether such people feel close to Judaism or not; what is

[7] *Esprit*, Paris, February 1953.

important is that moral rigour gives them a place in the ranks of those who pursue the messianic combat outlined by the Hebrew prophets. This combat is a challenge to a world living under the threat of totalitarian tyranny and is to be pursued side-by-side with Israel as an equal ally, no longer to be sympathized with or protected.

For those less well-informed and less politically aware, the risk, although rarely made explicit, may seem frightening indeed: Does the acceptance of a victorious Jewish state not mean putting up with Israel, the people of the law? The original source, so often stemmed and diverted but still present—will it not become a torrent, sweeping all away before it? In this sense the more absurd accusations launched against Israel (greed for territory, for instance, a wicked will to dominate the Arab world) are significant of a deep unease in the minds of those who make them. If that is so, the Golan Heights become something more than a few square miles of barren hillside—they are a thorn in the flesh. And the people who swear that the entrance to the Knesset in Jerusalem is surmounted with a map of the "Zionist State from the Nile to the Euphrates" are not necessarily liars; some of them are genuinely persuaded that they have seen this sight with their own eyes, even though they may never have set foot in Jerusalem (others even think the Knesset is in Tel Aviv!). We must resist the temptation to believe that people obsessed with the Devil have never really seen him.

I talk about "people" because I know of no specific term which would adequately cover this grab bag, ranging from pro-Arab neo-Nazis to pro-Palestinian left-wing Christians, all united by the great metaphysical fear. Within this collection are the "Jews in the other camp," whose tragic inability to accept themselves must be mentioned: for Otto Weininger, a Viennese anti-Semitic Jew, the result was folly and suicide; for the American Daniel Burros, a member of Rockwell's pro-Hitlerian party, suicide when his Jewish origins came to light. Faced by irrationality on this scale, it is hardly surprising that the pro-Israeli Left, deliberately keeping to what it considers logical arguments, should be so defenceless politically. It is a wonderful position, on the other hand, for anti-Zionist propaganda in its attempt to make Israel bear on every occasion the burden of proving its innocence while being perpetually presumed guilty.

The ups and downs of history being what they are, especially in a climate of permanent insecurity, Israel is no more guilty than any other state similarly placed. The existence of any organized state implies frustration for some and a certain degree of force. No matter how high its moral claims may be pitched, no state is always irreproachable or exempt from undesirable pressures. Joan of Arc was burnt in the name of the merciful Christ; Captain Dreyfus was degraded in the name of the honour of the French Army. Every state when threatened recognizes the right to act in accordance with what is called *raison d'Etat*. Is Israel above reproach? In Israel's case there are a flock of observers who would like this to be affirmed in order to be able to point the finger when, as inevitably happens, Israel proves open to criticism, in which event they will publish their findings with relish.

But in the eyes of the country's sworn enemies this is as nothing compared with the guilt of existing, especially from the date on which it emerged as a real state and with all the attributes of victory — "natural" frontiers, money apparently flowing in, and an army apparently unbeatable. In fact, these enemies cannot admit the existence of any purely Jewish territory at all, no matter how exiguous, nor any Jewish financial strength, even if the fruit of a natural solidarity, nor any Jew under arms. They feel themselves threatened by Jewish life as such, no matter what form it may take. The more so in that they are incapable of living at the same tempo as this resurrected people; capable only of carrying death into the other camp in fleeing the tasks they ought to be confronting. In the summer of 1968, a similar phenomenon was observable among the Soviet leaders, who were quite unable to accept the outburst of vitality in Prague.

The "Chosen People"

Israel resists the machinery of death, whether guided by folly or by *raison d'Etat*, within the limits of the possibilities available, and not in the name of some impossible, because absolute, moral code. During the "Black September" and again in the summer of 1976, Israel was the only country in which the *fedayeen* pursued by the soldiers of King Hussein and President Assad of Syria were offered refuge and medical care, which would seem to show the priority given to moral and humanitarian considerations in Jerusalem. I shall not of course claim that everything Israel does or may do will be beyond reproach. But Israeli public opinion, I believe, would not have allowed the government to close the frontier to exhausted and wounded men, whose lives would have been in danger had they been refused asylum. I believe that this feeling for the human has over the centuries sustained the hopes entertained by the Jewish people in the advent of an era when the inhuman would be abolished.

The Jewish people have always displayed extraordinary continuity in trying to bring God into life. I do not say that this people is incapable of violence or injustice, but I do maintain that messianism is a barrier against that which would compromise the coming of the Messiah. This is the sense in which we must interpret the idea of "election." The Chosen People are in reality the people who choose — choose to include God in life.

A choice of God means a choice of life, and not of any life — a life of responsibility. An exciting but painful adventure, a necessary dimension of which is misfortune and will remain so until the messianic hope is realized. An exemplary patience? No doubt, but above all else an enormous confidence, capable of rising superior to any blow that life may inflict. Without confidence, the Jews would long ago have ceased to exist, and the effects would have been felt by the whole of mankind. It is precisely this hope and this confidence which tyrannies have always set out to destroy. The only kind of hope which exists under such tyrannies is that of violent revolution, without any guarantee — as shown by bitter experience — that the morrow will be blessed by song and laughter, nor indeed that it will be blessed at all. The man who is animated by an unquenchable hope is the natural enemy of the tyrant. When an entire people, rather than an individual, is the bearer of hope, the tyrant's fury is all the greater.

Thus the attitude adopted towards Israel is a touchstone. It is no accident that the anti-Israeli governments and movements are opposed to any sign of strivings for greater freedom in the Soviet Union or Third World. Messianism is confidence which survives and resists, and is sometimes apparently triumphant. Then it is that fear becomes contagious.

Jerusalem as the Capital

Should there be any need for a date to be chosen for some future history book to mark the beginning of the great fear which is with us today, I would suggest 10 June 1967. On that day, the sixth in the Six-Day War, Israel and its people were suddenly perceived by the world as no longer perpetually vanquished or historically nonexistent, as had been the case before 1948; as no longer on the defensive, as in 1948; as no longer willing to display docility by surrendering the fruits of their victory, as in 1956 — but were for the first time in a position to look back on, and defend, a victory.

On that day, the barriers were swept away, an equilibrium was destroyed. Those who feared Judaism, however vaguely, felt that it was about to overthrow their idols. Also, unfortunately, a number of people who had previously proudly declared themselves the protectors of an oppressed and humiliated Israel changed sides overnight, for there is no satisfaction to be gained from protecting the victors. From that day onwards, because Israel exists and victoriously exists, all these people have entertained a deformed image of it, whatever the country may have done or not done, which Sadat's visit only partially corrected. One major stumbling block for those who think in this way is the fact that Israel should have proclaimed Jerusalem the capital of the state and established Jewish sovereignty there.

Israel retook the old section of the city half-way through the Six-Day War. But only after the final cease-fire did the event really produce a decisive impact. The outside world was forced to admit that something conclusive had come to pass, not just another shift in the back-and-forth of some eternal tug-of-war. In 1956, a desert had been conquered; in 1967, a city, *the* city.

It is because Edenists unconsciously believe that they alone are entitled to exercise total spiritual power that a Jewish protectorate over the holy places seems so full of menace. That menace was and is imaginary, but the immediate reaction showed the fear to be a real one.

On 29 August 1969, a demented Australian, a Protestant, tried to set fire to the El Aqsa mosque in Jerusalem. Anti-Semitism everywhere immediately echoed the hysterical reaction of the Moslem world, although the Jews themselves had no part in the affair. That some of the sound and fury was fed by the Christian churches, passionately divided among themselves with respect to Christian holy places, is unfortunately true, and might well induce Jews to reflect with some bitterness on the sentiments of those who abhor them for refusing the Christian revelation. In fact, for all the indignation, access to the holy places has never been so free as it has since 1967; more importantly, Jews are no longer refused access to their own holy places, as they had been between 1948 and 1967 (the Christian West remaining totally indifferent).

Edenism finds it difficult (even impossible) to accept the fact that Judaism, in recovering its capital, should have ceased to be divided and dismembered. No longer acephalous, it is now able to face its enemies with a recovered vigour. It now possesses the central brain it needs to manage the affairs of the Jewish nation.

Jerusalem is one example of the symbolic importance attached to capital cities in the course of history. The German occupation of Paris and then its liberation were events of symbolic significance, causing emotion throughout the world. But the fact that Königsberg, a purely German city and the home of Kant, or Vilna, a Polish-Jewish-Lithuanian town, should have been annexed by the Russians at about that time, and remain annexed today, seems not to impinge on anybody except those directly concerned because neither city had any status as a symbol.

Of all places which do possess such a status, Jerusalem is unique in being the "Celestial City," and not in literature alone. It represents, in the minds of men, a confused image of paradise on earth, the reign of justice and love—and not only for the religions of the Book. Apart from the other grudges the world nurses against the Jews, it is perhaps the supreme affront that they should have chosen this one city in which to end their eternal wanderings. One of the Devil's aims is to prevent the Just from entering Heaven; if the Jews have got there first, this can but be a maneuver by Satan himself.

The Manichaeism implicit in this situation is dramatic enough; we are back to the totem and taboo of primitive societies. A people condemned to eternal homelessness is guilty of nothing less than sacrilege in claiming a "holy place." Whenever possible, action must be taken to dispossess it. In 1948, when the Arab Legion occupied the Jewish area of Jerusalem, all its inhabitants were killed or expelled, its synagogues profaned and destroyed, its tombstones used to build latrines.

These are the facts of history, all too easily forgotten or denied because embarrassing. Any Jewish presence in Jerusalem can but appear a sacrilege to the post-Judaic faiths, whose constant endeavour it is to monopolize the sacred symbol. If, for the Marxist, this is not "obscurantism," it is because he has been marked, more than he likes to acknowledge, by the catechism rather than by *Das Kapital*. Hence an attempt will be made to forget or deny—for facts need denial—the entire past of the city. Firstly, that from the time of David onwards Jerusalem has always been the capital of the Jewish people (and of that people alone) even during the long centuries of occupation, as Paris remained the capital of France during the German occupation and would have remained such even had the occupation lasted centuries. To deny this means denying the figures which show that, despite massacre and expulsion, the majority of the population of Jerusalem has always been Jewish. And it would mean denying that both Christians and Moslems were perfectly content to leave the city to dilapidation and decay for centuries, beginning to display an anxious concern for its welfare only after the Jews had begun to make their presence felt. Why, incidentally, should they take such an interest in this city? The Christians have Rome and Canterbury, the Suni Moslems have Mecca and Medina (and the Sh'ite Moslems, Qom), whereas the Jews have this one city, a national capital and a religious symbol. Nevertheless, anti-Zionists are not deterred from organizing seminars and lectures on such themes as "Jerusalem, city of the Canaanities." This is about as realistic as calling Marseilles a Phoenician city to imply that it is not French. Such absurdities are professed only for Jerusalem. But they are believed and repeated and are used as a weapon against Israel.

An Idea of the Apocalypse

Many other dates and facts could be mentioned and given a coefficient of irrationality as a function of the fear they generate. One event, however, is singularly enlightening in this respect.

On 28 December 1968, in reprisal for an attack with loss of life on an El Al airplane in Athens, a small Israeli force alighted from helicopters at Beirut airport and destroyed thirteen Lebanese aircraft on the ground, the intention obviously being to make it quite plain to the Arabs that an air blockade of Israel (over and above the blockade of land routes already imposed) would not pass without reaction. We may also reasonably assume that the planners of this operation tried to avoid unnecessary loss of life.

Be that as it may, almost every government, and certainly those of all the major powers, reacted in a manner grossly out of proportion to the purpose of the operation or its results. In France, General de Gaulle used it as a pretext to declare a complete embargo on the export of arms to Israel. At the Security Council, Israel was *unanimously* condemned. That Arab terrorists had taken life in Athens was not even mentioned.

It is hardly possible to explain the intensity of these reactions without reference to the notions I have tried to define: Edenism, Manichaeism, the need for an ontological explanation of surface phenomena.

Anything Israel may do produces denunciations which go far beyond those produced by a similar action taken by another country. This was true of the Beirut affair, which, *although there were no victims,* produced a storm of indignation exceeding in violence even that elicited by the (very limited) Israeli penetration into South Lebanon in March 1978, indeed, exceeding the indignation produced by any other contemporary event. So much so that we are led to seek an explanation in the fact that for once in military history *there had been no loss of life*.

Such an operation could not but appear an impudent Jewish affront to the world of the Edenists. This world, which is not at all sentimental about death (in 1975 and 1976, in Beirut again, thousands of Christians were to be sacrificed, the Holy See remaining indifferent or at any rate refusing to take sides), must have seen something symbolic, and something of intolerable significance, in the wrecks left burning on the tarmac.

De Gaulle, who displayed such fury after the incident in Beirut, had shown no hesitation in ordering French troops into action at Bizerta in 1961, when 12,000 Tunisians lost their lives. In retrospect, however, it is clear that the blood shed on that occasion served no purpose whatsoever; France and Tunisia lost no time in establishing relations which would have suffered had not the dead been conveniently forgotten. The events in Beirut on that December day of 1968 were a lesson; they taught us that Jewish bullets, destroying the inanimate, carry more weight in history than any typically colonialist slaughter.

Incidentally, the enemies of the affluent society are probably quite right in criticizing it for the worship of the inanimate and the cult of the machine. Certainly a subsidiary reason for the fury roused by Beirut was the blow struck at this form of idolatry, a form denounced, with its cults, by the Hebrew prophets. Adoration of the machine, and notably of the motor vehicle, is characteristic of the neo-pagan age in which we live. Those who were so quick to shed tears of rage and indignation at the treatment meted out to these new idols were reacting like the worshippers of Baal when that deity was overthrown by iconoclastic monotheism. What was done in Beirut by that Israeli force must have seemed an act of revolution in every sense.

It is therefore not surprising that this event should have been felt to be the manifestation of a superhuman power, marking the final overthrow of barriers and idols which the Six-Day War had begun. The wicked power feared by the Edenists had suddenly appeared as an angel able to destroy matter without taking life. The angel's very success was a sign that the End was nigh. It was therefore more important than ever that this new force be refused access to Eden.

It may be surprising that I have chosen an example going as far back as December 1968. Why finish on this apocalyptic note? Since that time, the Israeli-Arab conflict has evolved. The Yom Kippur War, thanks above all to anti-Zionist propaganda, has effaced Israel's reputation for invincibility; the frontier along the Jordan has remained open, with increasing contacts between the Arab inhabitants on the two sides; the frontier between Israel and its unfortunate neighbour Lebanon has been opened in its turn and a *de facto* alliance entered into between Israel and a part of the people of that country; lastly, and above all, agreements have been entered into between Israel and Egypt which for the time being at least would seem to preclude recourse to force as a means of settling the conflict between them.

Despite these recent and important developments, I have deliberately emphasized reactions to the reconquest of Jerusalem and the Israeli commando attack on Beirut airport, both of them events especially revealing a way of thinking which has hitherto been obstinately resistant to change.

It is significant, to revert to some of the examples I have already quoted, that the contacts inaugurated by the President of Egypt between his country and Israel have aroused such ferocious hostility in his own camp, which continues to refuse recognition and discussions in any shape or form. It is significant, too, that the anti-Zionists see in the opening of the Lebanese frontier and the contacts between Israel and what is disparagingly referred to as the Lebanese "Right" no more than a sordid self-interested maneuver, it being self-evident, of course, that Israel is essentially incapable of a disinterested gesture and that any political alliance that country may contract or consolidate pursues an evil end (while the enemies of Israel are welcome to conclude whatever alliances they see fit). It is significant that talks between individual Israelis and Palestinians (if indeed they have taken place) are always clandestine and regularly disavowed by the PLO, as though, instead of being the only way out, such talks were a shameful compromise or an unavoidable recourse. The Rejectionist Front and its friends have been unyielding in their negation of Jewish national identity, constant in brandishing anathemas against the Jewish state and in attempts to isolate Israel (as shown by the protests made by Arab countries when Portugal established diplomatic relations with that country), and uncompromising in their threat to use that supreme economic weapon—oil—as an instrument of blackmail against the rest of the world while threatening the very survival (the point is essential and cannot be overlooked) of the Jews as a nation.

I emphasize once more, at the risk of appearing repetitive, that in these pages I express hostility to no enemy living within any definite frontiers. Anti-Zionism, the form which anti-Jewish feeling takes today, is a will-o'-the-wisp, now here, now there, according to circumstances, and able to cause an anti-Jewish explosion in any Western country (where anti-Jewish feeling is endemic), even though matters should improve in the Middle East. A flame the more dangerous in that it often appears to have been extinguished, only to flare up again with renewed force at the first spark.

Freedom to Be

I would myself tend to fall into the trap of Edenism if I tried to find a solution to the problem of history. I have depicted history, and those who make it, the way I have experienced it in relation to the Jewish people, and to myself. Only when the Edenists fully understand how alienated they are, and act accordingly, will they be free. This is, perhaps, my way of sustaining belief in the messianic era.

Should we, in this respect at any rate, try to change the world? If we were in so doing performing a duty, it would be of little moment if our efforts proved vain. We can fight with no illusions and even so prepare the advent of the messianic era. But what is the price to be paid, and how and when can we be sure that no further calls will be made upon us?

The merit of the Greeks was to have shown that human fate is tragic. Where the Edenists go wrong is in denying the evidence, in endeavouring to find and even to impose a solution where perhaps none is possible.

But hope, too, forms part of man's lot, a point understood by the civilizations of the Book. Hope based on the Book, thus on a single civilization. For despite all the obvious differences between Edenisms and Judaism, the latter has nevertheless exerted a powerful influence on the philosophical, political, and social thought of our time.

An attempt to disallow any expression of religious views other than one's own, when one is convinced that one has the key to a solution of the world's problems, is bound to lead to violence, and violence is no abstraction—it means, in concrete terms, death, destruction, blood and tears. I am aware, too, that while violence may sometimes be a necessary expedient to avoid something worse, it can never establish its own legitimacy. How many tears must be shed to inaugurate an era in which there will be no more weeping? And, if paid for at too high a price, would such an era deserve to be called messianic? Should we not have to start all over again? And if this is the case, how can we avoid doing the same as before?

Is, therefore, the messianic hope nothing but a consoling dream, impossible of realization? What use is morality if this is so? Although the Messiah can come at any time, the wait seems endless. Perhaps—I do not know—messianism is to be valued for the constant daily effort it encourages, whether or not the Messiah ever comes. What is important is to observe the survival and the force of the messianic hope and the fears it arouses.

Anti-Zionists, like traditional anti-Semites, see only the reverse side of the coin in Jewish history—the reaction not the act, the accident not the cause, the wastage not the process of creation. In this they display a lack of human understanding and also an inability to think dialectically—shortcomings from which they are the first to suffer. The way in which, to salve their consciences and in the interest of their policies, they picture the Jew as a sordid, guilty "Zionist" freezes their ability to think and feel. The freedom to exist which they refuse me prevents them from seeing the world as it is. Their reasoning is infantile, their information inadequate, their scale of values absurd in that one Palestinian equals 1,000 Kurds or 10,000 Balts or Armenians—and how many Nagas or Tibetans? (A scale in which an Afghan, incidentally, counts for nothing.) The anti-Zionist is not interested in the sufferings of these other peoples and takes no trouble to find out about them, or about many others in revolt against the imperialisms he is all too ready to praise. The free Jew, the Israeli, he is completely unable to understand.

* * *

Time, as science tells us, is the fourth dimension. It is a flexible concept when it comes to imagination, but it does not take care of our concerns. Another is misfortune, which underlines our path from the cradle to the grave. It may be the dominant dimension of a whole people, and this is the case today for peoples colonized by those who were once colonized themselves or by Arabs, Russians, or Chinese. It was once true of the Jews, from Jerusalem lost to Jerusalem regained. They have recovered control over their own fate. Those who persist in refusing them recognition are refusing their own freedom. They cannot admit that at last all should have a choice. They do not want any challenge to Eden as they see it, an Eden which suits them and their beliefs, an Eden they are ready to offer and indeed to impose on others with the satisfying feeling that they are acting in the common good.

What I have called "Edenism" is, historically speaking, no more than imperialism behind a benevolent facade. Let those to whom the offer is made rebel against a police state and everything is called in question, including the peace of mind of those who direct and of those who accept it. What would happen if the Armenians were to rise in revolt and throw off Turkish and Soviet hegemony? If other non-independent peoples were to follow the Jewish example, there would be an end to tutelary tyranny.

The Israelis face a total risk: they can have security without peace, or perhaps — it is not certain — by extensive concessions, peace without security. Their enemies are confronted by no such dilemma. Assuming the solution least favourable to them — i.e., a greater Israel finally recognized within its historical natural frontiers — Sinai would be returned to Egypt (this is now being done, even though it was occupied by Egypt only by virtue of an arbitrary division of the Ottoman Empire) and the Palestinians would be included in Transjordan, in which they already represent a majority.

As to messianism in the Jewish world of today . . . That the witness it bears should be so hesitant and incomplete, that Judaism, at one and the same time armoured against certain trends and dominated by them, should be so little aware of the spiritual significance of its mission, is another misfortune on top of so many others.

What, then, I may be asked, is the answer? A political analysis does not necessarily throw up a solution and is certainly not conducive to naive optimism. No more than the next man can I claim to have found the answer, although I am bold — or modest? — enough to realise this.

This in no way diminishes the responsibility of those countries which, having adopted a resolution that virtually calls for the spiritual destruction of a nation, have given their blessing in advance to any crime such as the murder of the six young people in Jerusalem and created a climate favourable for some future attempt at genocide. Even in those countries which declined to associate themselves with that resolution, the authorities have constantly yielded to blackmail. In France, the Barre government arrested the notorious terrorist Abu Daud only to release him immediately for fear of reprisals. For the same reason the Venezuelan terrorist "Carlos" is allowed to cross frontiers with impunity. Italy alone provides a dozen ignoble examples; here, the authorities quite simply released, without formality, two Arabs convicted of having, in August 1972, seduced two young English girls on their way to Israel, offering them "presents" which hid delayed-action bombs.

The obstinacy with which very serious threats to Israel and the Jewish people are regularly played down in the West goes further than the unconvincing argument that an Israeli act of self-defence is *ipso facto* an aggression. An attempt is being made to credit the idea that such threats are nonexistent, because Israel does not exist; a non-being cannot be destroyed, nor can there be condemnation for murder if there is no possible victim. These tactics are not so different from those followed in the Soviet Union, in whose newspapers anti-Semitic (anti-Zionist) caricatures depict Jews in a form so abject that they no longer resemble human beings. Similarly, it will be asserted that there were no victims of Hitler's massacres, since no such massacres took place.[8]

The same premises serve when an author can write, for instance, that "any reference to Jewish martyrdom is suspect when the aim is to find a legal basis for the political rights of Israel."[9] Thus, for the Jews, but for them alone, historical precedents are disallowed.

Observe again that the very same people who find it intolerable that a small minority of Arabs should live under Israeli control find it entirely natural that eastern Jews should have lived under Moslem rule for centuries. They find it natural that the Jews who have resurrected a nation should be called upon to take their place in a so-called democratic Arab State, tolerated at best and utterly dependent on the goodwill of a majority swayed by whatever wind happens to be blowing in the Arab world. Such tolerance is in fact another name for intolerance—of the Jews, of the Palestinians, even of reality.

The freedom to be Jewish is thus concomitant with the freedom to be. For centuries, it was possible to assert this freedom only on shaky or illusory grounds, owing to an absence of choice and a constantly challenged future. Israel reborn represents the freedom of choosing one's freedom, and not only for the Jewish people.

What is more, in the face of all the dictatorships, but also in the face of all the paradises promised by Heaven or history, it should be an affirmation of man's inalienable right to be free without fear.

I make one last mention of those pathetic figures who, at loggerheads with themselves, are so prominent in the campaign against Israel—the alienated Jews. I try not to think of them with dislike or contempt; rather, I think of them with sadness and a touch of anguish, of the kind one feels in looking back at one's own irreparable mistakes. There are failings which can never be repaired in this life. I think, for instance, of a certain ex-Stalinist who in criminal blindness helped to

---

[8] See Paul Berman, "Crackpot History and the Right to Lie", in *Village Voice*, New York, 10–16 June 1981.

[9] From *Le Nouvel Observateur*, but much else on similar lines could be quoted, notably from the French press.

secure the condemnation of his dearest friend (who miraculously escaped death) and suffers from the obsessive fear of one day meeting this symbol of his shame. Crime against oneself and one's inner integrity may perhaps be less serious in its consequences. No doubt my poor parents were unable to foresee what in their time was hardly imaginable; no doubt none of the millions of Jews done to death could have foreseen their fate. But today, now that the unimaginable has become part of history, the Jews who allow themselves to be victims of illusion are inviting destruction.

* * *

Is human destiny a tragedy? In any event, it cannot be mapped out in advance. What is tragic is the course of past history, which stops right here and now. The future is in the image of God, a God who may be a gamble. In other words, the future may also turn out in the image of man. If, from the human standpoint, life is the only true absolute, then Evil cannot also be an absolute. The point is to believe in Dubček despite Husak, in the deceased Allende despite the living Pinochet, in Sadat despite everything. Moreover, the messianic type of hope knows that it runs the risk of having to redouble its efforts incessantly, like a hapless but infinitely wealthy gambler caught in an endless martingale. The game is never lost as long as the wealth of hope is inexhaustible, and one knows that the only miracle is faith in the miracle, a miracle which would make of God's creature a creator in God's image, capable of being free without perverting freedom by means of lies and calumny simply because others are different, and by a rejection of freedom and therefore life itself.

The fact remains that the idea of God is not so easily consigned to oblivion. In his collection of aphorisms *On Religion* Nietzsche wrote: "The Jews—the worst of peoples," and four lines further on: "God completely superfluous." It is not an accident that the most stubbornly monotheistic of peoples should be the first to attract the wrath of those who would have done with God.

But I have no more truck with those who theorize about the death or defeat of God than with the zealots of God triumphant. Rather I would pay tribute to that mythology from which so many philosophies are drawn (it is also a root of the world in which we live), I like to think of Prometheus as being able, unaided, to cast off his chains, and to imagine that from then on no vultures will be sent by

Heaven to pick his entrails. He is no longer willing to await deliverance by some deity. No more than you or I does he foresee the future. But he knows that the gods, still able to inflict the most fearful torments, no longer, thanks to him, possess the privilege of fire.

He knows, too, that those gods, like him, like all of us, are cast in human form.

POSTSCRIPT

Anwar Sadat was assassinated on 6 October 1981, as this book was going to press. In the belief that what I have written ought to remain unaffected by contingencies, I prefer to make no changes in the text.

A few days after the assassination, the press reported the following comment by Colonel Qaddafi: "A traitor has got what was coming to him. He is now dead and buried. Having lived like a Jew, he has died like one."

Sadat's assassins wished to eliminate the man who had come out in favour of friendship with Israel; they wished to wreck the peace of which, with Menahem Begin, he had been the architect. Those—and unfortunately they are not a few—who encouraged, armed, or applauded Sadat's murderers are at one and the same time the enemies of peace, of Egypt and of Israel. Happy that more blood should have been shed, their satisfaction would be complete if the people of Egypt were to rejoin the rejectionist front, and if, once more, the Jewish people were to lose their national identity.

This hostility to peace and friendship between the two peoples has been evident all along. What, in addition, we now see clearly displayed, is the transfer of a murderous hatred of Jews, and of the national entity founded by them, to the man who dared offer the hand of friendship to the Jewish people and the Israeli nation. Hitler was equally contemptuous of the Jews and the "Verjüdeten"—those who might have come under Jewish influence or dared say a word in favour of the Jews. Those who applaud Sadat's assassins equally fail to distinguish between the Jews and their friends. They were determined to eliminate this Jew.